Remedial And Surrogate
Parenting

A Resource for Parents, Teachers, and Childcare Services

Like footprints each child is different!

Hollis L. Green, ThD, PhD

GREEN WINE™
FAMILY BOOKS

REMEDIAL AND SURROGATE PARENTING
A Resource for Parents, Teachers, and Childcare Services
Copyright © 2013 by Hollis L. Green

Library of Congress Control Number 2013943610
Green, Hollis L., 1933 –
Remedial and Surrogate Parenting
A Resource for Parents, Teachers, and Childcare Services

ISBN 978-1-935434-48-1
        Subject Codes and Description: 1: FAM010000. Family and
        Relationships: Parenting – Child Rearing; 2; FAM 042000 Family
        and Relationships: Parenting – Step Parenting; 3; FAM034000.
        Family and relationships: Parenting - General

Cover design by Barton Green
Author's photograph by Carie Thompson Olfori: www.cariephoto@gmail.com

The Press does not have ownership of the contents of a book; this is the
author's work and the author owns the copyright. All theory, concepts,
constructs, and perspectives are those of the author and not necessarily
the Press. They are presented for open and free discussion of the issues
involved. All comments and feedback should be directed to the Email:
comments4author@aol.com and they will be forwarded to the author for
response.

Published by
GreenWine Family Books™
A Division of GlobalEdAdvancePRESS
www.globaledadvance.org
www.gea-books.com

This book is dedicated with appreciation to

SUBESH AND DEBRA RAMJATTAN

Who, understanding that each child was different,
faithfully followed faith-based principles and
unselfishly invested resources and energy
to build bridges of hope and care for
disadvantaged children.

The long life of Benjamin Spock (1903-1998) and the popularity of his seminal book, *The Common Sense Book of Baby and Child Care,* published in 1946 (with revisions up to 2004) by Duell, Sloan & Pearce, speaks to the urgent search by parents and surrogate caregivers for assistance with the problems of growing children. His first book was a bestseller and sold more than 50 million copies in 49 languages.

Dr. Spock's message to others was simple and straight forward "You know more than you think you do." Parents and surrogate caregivers must use their common sense in dealing with the nurturing and development of children.

TABLE OF CONTENTS

Surrogate childcare is not a basket of bad apples that need to be culled from society. Rather it is a cradle of socialization filled with precious fruit of the womb picked prematurely from the tree of life.

Just like footprints each child is different and age-specific care is required to preserve them for a positive future.

Present circumstance has created a social environment that reduces the influence of the home and increases the role of the "global village" in raising and educating children. The primary responsibility for producing and preparing a child for adult responsibility, rests on the biological parents. Children are in the custodial care of biological parents for only a few years. With the miracle of birth, some see a child as a gift from God and suggest that a child is entrusted to parental custody. In this custodial arena, even parents are surrogates and will be accountable to a Higher Power and the global village for the nurturing of the child. When parents fail to act responsibly in bringing up their children, the burden falls on the social order. Those individuals and systems that provide surrogate care for children will be accountable to society. Yet, assistance is available through divine intervention and personal devotion. Sacred scripture is clear that one should be patiently focused on the outcome of their effort rather than the difficulty:

> 3. Knowing that your painful trial brings you assurance, trust and works patience. 4. But let suffering have her complete labor and make something of you, that you may be complete in all respects, without defect or omission and whole undivided, and unbroken. 5. **If any of you lack wise judgment, let him express the craving by words to God, that gives to all men liberally, and does not defame, chide or snatch away your joy,** and it shall be given him. 6. But let him ask in faith, nothing wavering for he that shows doubt or indecision is like a wave of the sea driven with the wind and tossed. 7. Let not that man think that he shall receive anything of the Lord. 8. A two-spirited man is unsettled and wavering in all his direction, position or manner. (James 1:2-8 EDNT)

Providence ordered three
Basic institutions: the family,
Community authority, and
Faith-Based Organizations.

The three institutions
are interrelated and
cannot survive alone.

Divine
Influence

FAITH-BASED
ORGANIZATIONS

FAMILY
GROUP

COMMUNITY
SOCIETY

INDIVIDUALS
(ORGANISM

Three Basic Institutions- Each institution is related to the
individual: the Family PRODUCES individuals; the Community
PROTECTS individuals, and Faith-Based Organizations
PRESERVES individuals in the context of the family and the
community.

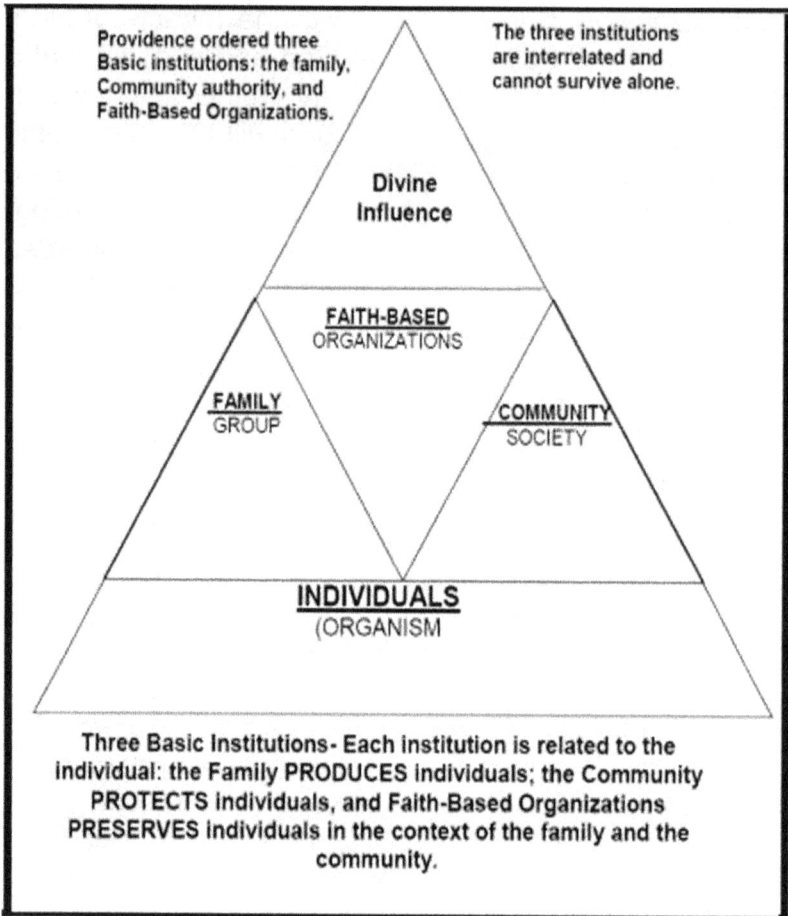

See page 30 for further explanation of this diagram

Like footprints each child is different!

This text is a suitable syllabus for **Human Development: The Early Years (Birth to Twenty)** -- A study of physical, emotional, cognitive, social, moral/spiritual, and personality factors as they influence development through the life cycle stages (Birth to Twenty). It is directed to parents, grandparents, and caregivers in custodial situations, such as children's homes, orphanages, child shelters, state and agency operated facilities, and the host of foster-care families. These families have been willing to take up the slack and provide childcare and nurture for a disadvantaged child who through no fault of the child was orphaned, abandoned, neglected or abused and were placed in the custodial care of individuals other than birth parents or members of the extended family. It is affirmed by the author that this syllabus is suitable for use in Family Life Education courses that require NCFR Criteria #3.

The USA based National Council on Family Relations (NCFR Minneapolis, MN) sponsors the only program to certify family life educators internationally. The Certified Family Life Educator (CFLE) program encourages applications from all professionals internationally with subject work and experience in family life education including formal teaching, community education, curriculum and resource development, health care, military family support, counseling, and ministry.

Clear your calendar.

Turn off your cell.

Open your heart!

Turn on all three ears:

the two on your head and the one in your h-ear-t.

Listen, analyze, and act.

You can make a difference

in the life of a child.

Like footprints each child is different!

INTRODUCTION

FOOTPRINTS TO FOOTSTEPS

If the old adage be true that the hand that rocks the cradle rules the world, all that is needed is a well-trained hand to rock that cradle, and eventually point those wandering feet in the right direction. Then those who guide the footsteps of growing children will be building the Kingdom of Heaven. It was the Master Himself who said, "Permit the children to come to me, and do not hinder them: for of such is the kingdom of God." (Luke 18:16 EDNT) Since ancient scripture was clear that training up children in the proper way would provide assurance that when they are older they would not depart from such guidance, all that is needed is a well-trained hand to rock that cradle and eventually point those wandering feet in the right direction.

Surrogate childcare is not a basket of bad apples that need to be culled from society. Rather it is a cradle of socialization filled with precious fruit of the womb picked prematurely from the tree of life. Just like footprints, each child is different and age-specific care is required to preserve them for a positive future. Certainly the children have their share of trouble and need a happy place to enjoy food, fun, friends and room to grow.

It is reported that Mark Twain once said, "Laughter is the Hand of God on a troubled world." An ancient proverb dealt with both sides of this issue, "A merry heart doeth good like a medicine, but a broken spirit drieth the bones. (Proverbs 17:22) This is a noble goal. The challenging arena of custodial care is filled with committed service providers who not only supply remedial and surrogate parenting, but the best of them do so in an atmosphere of laughter; applying the medicine of a merry heart to the dry bones and broken spirit of disadvantaged children.

There is a relationship between the attitude, knowledge, and behavior of caregivers in remedial and surrogate parenting and the quality of custodial care for orphaned, abused, neglected, or abandoned children. This book is an effort to assure a positive and professional attitude among parents and others in custodial care, to provide sufficient knowledge of remedial development, and to provide basic guidance as to personal and professional behavior necessary to make parenting work in the home and with needy children in the custodial arena. The book can be both a study and a reference guide for parents and personnel working in children's homes, and foster parents who pick up the slack in society when custodial care is not sufficient or government agencies are slow to respond to the needs of children.

Objectives for Parenting and Childcare

1. Create a home environment conducive to learning that promotes growth, mutual respect and trust among children and caregivers.

2. Structure childcare services to educate and develop children giving priority to behavioral and learning needs of all children.

3. Provide structures, learning resources, technology and processes designed to motivate and engage children in

learning activities for development to prepare them for the real world of work and family.

4. Develop a tutoring/learning process that permits self-directed, individualized, face-to-face, and classroom learning in real life situations with dialog/support systems and technology suitable for children.

5. Strive for multicultural awareness with a broad exchange of teaching/learning experience across cultural and ethnic boundaries.

6. Partner with social and welfare systems to produce meaningful services for childcare and development in areas of need.

7. Work with the Schools and Child Protection Agencies to establish quality parenting and childcare skills and train qualified childcare workers to meet the needs of the children and the community.

The road to custodial care is paved with both good intentions and negative conditioning. Some see the problem and do nothing. Others recognize the difficulty and do little. Still others see the impact of a dysfunctional family and a troubled community on the children and build a bridge of hope. When children walk across the bridge of hope, they find a safe village where they can live and grow, but negative conditioning in the previous environment becomes a formidable barrier to remedial and surrogate parenting in the custodial arena. This must be understood to accomplish the process of remedial development in special needs children. Negative conditioning and procrastination are also problems for those providing childcare; past occurrences in their own lives are sometimes projected on the child. Child-rearing or providing care and upbringing of children requires special skills, qualities, experience, and responsibilities to teach and care for a child in a safe environment. Procrastination denies or delays positive action and permits the previous negative conditioning to fester and aggravate the positive aspects of custodial care.

Negative Conditioning

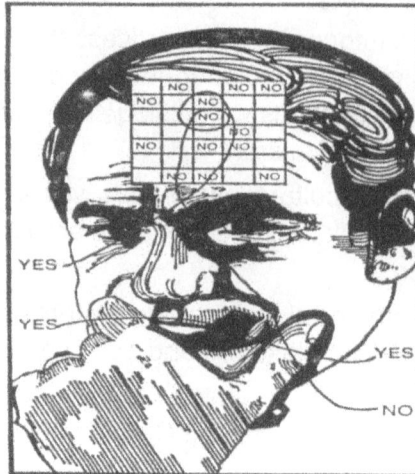

Figure 1

It would be helpful for parents and custodial workers to understand the meaning of key words used in this book to establish the structure and parameters of childcare.

Operational Definitions for Key Terms

Abandoned – the abdication of personal responsibility for a child left behind for others to provide care and support

Abused – the physical, psychological, or sexual maltreatment of a child including all illegal, improper, or harmful practices

Attitude – the predisposition to act in a negative or positive manner in a given situation and a tendency to respond in a given way to agent or factor that provokes interest or response

Behavior – the way one responds to a specific set of conditions that produces goal-directed activity of the caregiver and the child

Blended Families – is where both parents have children from a previous relationship.

Child – a young human being between birth and puberty

Children's Services - are non-profit social service agencies that provide foster care, adoption, and services that are culturally sensitive to children, youth and families. The goal is to maximize the strength of the family by delivering services and resources that promote self-discipline, initiative, and independence for children and parents. The surrogate services provided are those the family is unable or unwilling to provide.

Custodial – relating to the legal custody of and responsibility for the nurturing and guardianship of a child

Foster Care -- to provide a child with care and upbringing by someone other than a blood-relative through a program by an approved agency which allows surrogate parents, referred to as foster parents, to care for minor children removed for cause from their biological home. The meaning of "foster" is to promote the growth and development of a child and prepare them for reunification with their natural family or get them ready for adoption and meaningful citizenship.

Knowledge – the level of familiarity with the facts about both the child and the process of remedial and surrogate parenting

Neglected – to fail to receive the proper or required care and attention to a child because of carelessness, inability, or indifference

Orphaned — a child who has been deprived of parental care (orphan literally means *"without a father"*).

Parenting – the experiences, skills, qualities, and responsibilities involved in being a legal guardian and in teaching and/or caring for a child

Remedial – acting as a remedy or solution to a child's problems, including behavioral and learning difficulties

Stepfamily – is a family where one parent has children that are not related to the other parent. The unrelated partner in childcare becomes a surrogate parent.

Surrogate – taking the place of another as a substitute or replacement

It may be better to invest in children
than in the stock market.

Like footprints each child is different!

CHAPTER ONE

THE HARSH WORLD AND CHILDREN

From the traumatic moment of birth to the jolting reality of everyday life situations, children face a cruel and insensitive world. Much of the neglect and abuse directed at children comes from a dysfunctional family environment. The subtle clash between the forces of ignorance and abandonment of natural affection for one's offspring is often seen as a normal part of human existence. Because of moral decadence, many of the world's children live in the shadow of despair and suffer physical, mental, and sexual abuse. The light of human decency is consumed by moral darkness. The corrupting forces of evil work beneath the surface of world order to create slavery, child labor, lack of educational opportunity, and unsafe neighborhoods and family units.

Although discord is evident everywhere, many choose to ignore the obvious. The eyes of some have become accustomed to the lingering moral darkness, which causes limited vision and creates a false sense of security; consequently, they are unaware of and unprepared for the reality of neglected, abused, and abandoned children.

Battle Lines Have Been Drawn

Nonetheless, the battle lines have been drawn and the forces of evil are in rank and ready to destroy the nuclear family - the remaining influence of a moral society. There is obvious weakness in the family unit and the disgrace and tragedy of helpless children suffering because of neglect by adults. Some have developed a strategic attack plan to protect children by legal means; others have developed custodial care facilities that assume legal custody of children and assume responsibility for nurturing and guardianship. These facilities employ remedial and surrogate parents who replace previous guardians and act responsibly to remedy or solve a child's behavior and developmental difficulties. By providing a safe and secure place to grow and develop, children in custodial care have a much brighter future.

The Awakening Force of Hope

The twilight of morality may be eclipsed by the darkness of the times, but beneath the despair of children there is the awakening force of indestructible hope. Some are building bridges of hope to reach dysfunctional families and abused children. Others are volunteering to support the cause financially. Still others are the responsibility of custodial caregivers to awaken hope in the hearts, minds, and bodies of needy children. This hope brings with it the power of a scared responsibility. Those who take the hand of a child and walk across the bridge of hope become a vital part of the strategy to achieve the moral high ground for the children.

Not only do evil forces assault individual families, there seems to be an all-out warfare against human decency, ethics and faith-based morality or anything that hints at the essential elements of a moral heritage. As drunkenness and drug abuse increase, as the papers and the 24-7 news cycle are filled with story after story of child abuse, while the legal forces appear to be impotent to enforce the laws already on record, it is time to declare war on the forces of child neglect, abuse, and abandonment. This is not the time to feel powerless. Each one must work to build bridges of hope for the children. How can this be accomplished?

The "power of one" can accomplish much when the cause is right. Divine intervention will make the task physically possible. Together we can create a safe environment for the children and find a quality childcare workforce to do the necessary remedial and surrogate parenting to give needy children a positive future.

The Human Condition

The early days of the young and helpless have been full of trouble since the Serpent beguiled Eve, and Adam disobeyed the divine command. From the description of Job's trouble in Scared Writings, to the front-page news stories and 24-hour television programming, it is clear that modern life is not a bed of roses for children. When the innocent are born to mothers who abuse alcohol and drugs, when biological fathers are absent and take no responsibility for the children who are the product of their selfish behavior, it is time for us to wage moral warfare against the forces of neglect and abuse that plague the children. There must be a clear and formal declaration of war against moral delinquency to adequately mobilize the people to build bridges of hope for the children. It is clearly moral failure that complicates the troubled situations for children.

When parents permit their children to be taught in a school system where science is more powerful than morality, where evolution has replaced creation, and where man is little more than an advanced animal, it is no wonder some brutish and degrading behavior is justified by society and immoral acts are downplayed and explained in terms of sickness or upbringing. Somehow we must break through the bondage of abandonment and build a bridge of hope that will provide a safe and secure place for children to grow and have a positive future.

Destroy the Children -- Defeat the Nation

The forces of evil seek to destroy the family unit and thus destroy the children. In the ancient days of Job, the people came "to present themselves before the Lord: and the evil one presented himself as an Angel of Light. When God asked the lord of evil where he had been, the great tempter's answer was simply, "From going to and fro in the earth, and from walking up and down in it." Following this encounter Job's great test came. (Job 1:6-8) Good people will be tested, but responsible action is required to save the children. The forces of evil are still roaming the earth seeking to destroy families and particularly children through careless parenting and deficient childcare that flagrantly violates accepted standards of decency. Evil is an active force around the world seeking to destroy any moral environment. We may not clearly understand how, but those who care about children must launch a strategic offensive against the forces that would destroy the family unit and the present generation. Damage the children -- desecrate the family! Corrupt the family – destroy the nation!

Strengths

There is strength in numbers, safety in community, and triumph in teamwork. To utilize the strength gained from the awareness of the plight of the children, more must be done to educate and equip parents and the caregivers to do the necessary remedial and surrogate parenting. Also, more must be done to inform the general public how they can assist the work of building bridges of hope and custodial villages for needy and desperate children. There is strength in agreement of purpose, and power in unity of action. We must work together to meet the challenge of abused, neglected, and abandoned children. Can you hear the cry for deliverance by the children? Can you hear the simple prayers of children; the silent screams in the night of a child without hope?

A Child's Simple Prayer

Prayer is best defined as "the sincere desire of the heart." There is a story of a small boy on his way to a rural school on the day of examination. He was anxious and decided to pray but did not know how. So he knelt by the side of the road near a fence corner and began saying A, B, C, D, etc. over and over. A man came along and heard the noise and asked the boy what he was doing. His answer, "I am praying. I have exams today." The man said you are not praying, you are just repeating the ABC's. The boy replied, "Sir, God is smart. He can make words out of ABC's!"

Delay of Total Deliverance

John Newton, master of a slave ship, encountered a divine emancipation he called his "great deliverance" after praying during a storm at sea (1748). Continuing in the slave trade after this experience, Newton began to change his attitude, and slaves under his care were treated humanely. Yet this change was not sufficient to satisfy a changed heart. He returned home, became a minister in the Church of England, and wrote many religious songs. For a weekly service, Newton wrote "amazing grace" and sang it to a tune he probably learned from the humming of African slaves. The first publication of Amazing Grace was in 1779 three decades after his life changing experience. The original verse was:

Amazing grace! (how sweet the sound)
That sav'd a wretch like me!
I once was lost, but now am found,
Was blind, but now I see.

Why such a long delay before Newton could clearly see the need for change? Social change comes slowly. Even when good people see the light and realize that a societal problem exists, the solution is often delayed for decades. The John Newton story is of a changed man who delayed positive action relative to a divinely revealed human need. It took a long time to change the agenda and act appropriately to stop the slave trade. After his heart was changed, his mind developed in a moral direction, and eventually he was able to execute positive acts toward the people he had wronged.

Newton's words and music still speak volumes today for anyone who will listen. The words and music provide hope that constructive change will come. The question is "Where, when and with whom will it begin?" Try this exercise: 1. Sing the tune of Amazing Grace using only the A,B, C's for the words. Let the silent prayer of abused and neglected children be heard. God is smart; he can make words out of those ABC's. 2.Try closing your eyes and humming the tune to Amazing Grace: listen for the moan and cry of a helpless and frightened child. It could change your attitude.

Sufficient inspiration could be gained to change your behavior. You could take the hand of a child and lead them across a bridge of hope. Rescue a child and save a life. Care for a child and nurture the nation! Value the nation and care for the children and the homeland will be a safe and secure environment for the children to grow and mature and make a constructive contribution to society.

It can be done! You can be part of the solution by not being part of the problem. What can you do new? What can you do different? What can you do better? What will you do now?

Since love may be an allusion that adults are different, it becomes clear that love declares that all children have the same needs. Whenever and wherever an individual deals with a child not their biological progeny, they are involved in remedial and surrogate parenting. This includes the teaching profession, the faith-based groups that deal with children, the welfare system and governmental children's services, stepparents, blended families, those involved in foster care, and social and childcare workers in a custodial environment.

> Children are a gift from God; they are his reward. Children born to a young man are like sharp arrows to defend him. Happy is the man who has his quiver full of them. That man shall have the help he needs when arguing with his enemies. (Psalms 127:3-5 TLB)

The childcare arena is a cradle
of socialization where children are assisted
in gaining skills required to function
successfully in society.
It is a place touched by the Hand of God
for the growth and development of children.

Like footprints each child is different!

CHAPTER TWO

CONCERN FOR CHILDREN

The Case for Individual Care

Historically, one sees clear evidence that divine intervention lovingly arranged for the care and nurturing of children. The fact that it takes two to conceive a child is evidence that the Creator intended both mother and father to be involved in the bringing up of a child. A child was to be **produced**, sheltered, and nurtured in a nuclear family, **protected** and developed in a constituted community, and **preserved** in the context of both family and community under the influence of a faith-based entity to be adequately prepared to make a contribution to society. Each entity was initiated for the good of the individual. When some part or all of this structure fails, by default a child is left to the wiles of the world, left at grandma's house, placed in custodial care, or left to the streets to fend for themselves.

The growth of a multicultural society in many parts of the world complicated the welfare of children. The existence of groups with different ethnic, religious, or political backgrounds within one society has brought about conflict, war, famine, political upheaval, and forced the immigration of some who were seeking a better life for their children. The migration often separated the nuclear family and the extended family. Many children lost the wholesome influence of mature grandparents and other members of their extended family.

The British Isles were once a WASP community (White-Anglo-Saxon-Protestant), but now through immigration has become a multicultural society. At one time the sun never went down on the British Empire because the kingdom stretched around the globe and included many different kinds of people and ethnic groups who could claim British passports. During hard times this produced an influx of immigration to England that totally changed the nature of English society. The children suffer the most!

Europe has recently seen an influx of immigration that totally changed the historic orientation of their society. Before, each country was invested with a national pride and identity, now they have a pluralistic concept of community called the European Union and the moral values and society standards have drastically changed to a standard of the lowest common denominator. The children no longer have a clear identity or connection to the past anchors of faith and family.

The United States of America began as an immigrant nation and has become a pluralistic society. Having a large land mass with pockets of race and ethnic-related communities, the country needed population and workers and invited immigration from around the world. America obviously wanted the minorities of the world to come and enjoy the blessings of liberty. This was done in good faith not realizing the damage that immigration brings to the nuclear and extended family. There was no understanding as to the impact of a multicultural society on the children. The desire was clear and the intent was good, but the impact on the children has been negative. Pluralism caused the separation of faith-based entities and the state; it created a multicultural view of morality which brought a diversity of views rather than a single approach and diluted the spirit of individual freedom. Yet the clearly expressed message on the Statue of Liberty still speaks to the general problems of the world. All citizens should be aware of the plight of poor and persecuted, especially the children. Every American, many of whom had immigrant or refugee ancestors who had entered through the Golden door, should know and appreciate the message of Mother Liberty:

Give me your tired, your poor, Your huddled masses yearning to breathe free, the wretched refuse of your teeming shore; Send these, the homeless, tempest-tossed to me, I lift my lamp beside the Golden door!

The rum-slave trade and the plantation system created the pluralism of the Western World. The Carbibbean, tropical paradise, has not escaped the plague of pluralism and all the ramifications for social policy and speculation. The breakdown of the nuclear family, the weakening of community morality, and the powerlessness of faith-based entities to make a moral difference has played havoc with the children.

Here is a custodial care manifesto, a declaration of concern, for the abandoned, neglected, and abused children. Read it; digest it; live it; love it.

The Surrogate Declaration

Give us your neglected or abandoned children,
The abused ones who ache for relief,
Across the bridge of hope through the love gate;
They will find a safe place to live and grow!

Understanding the Childcare Process

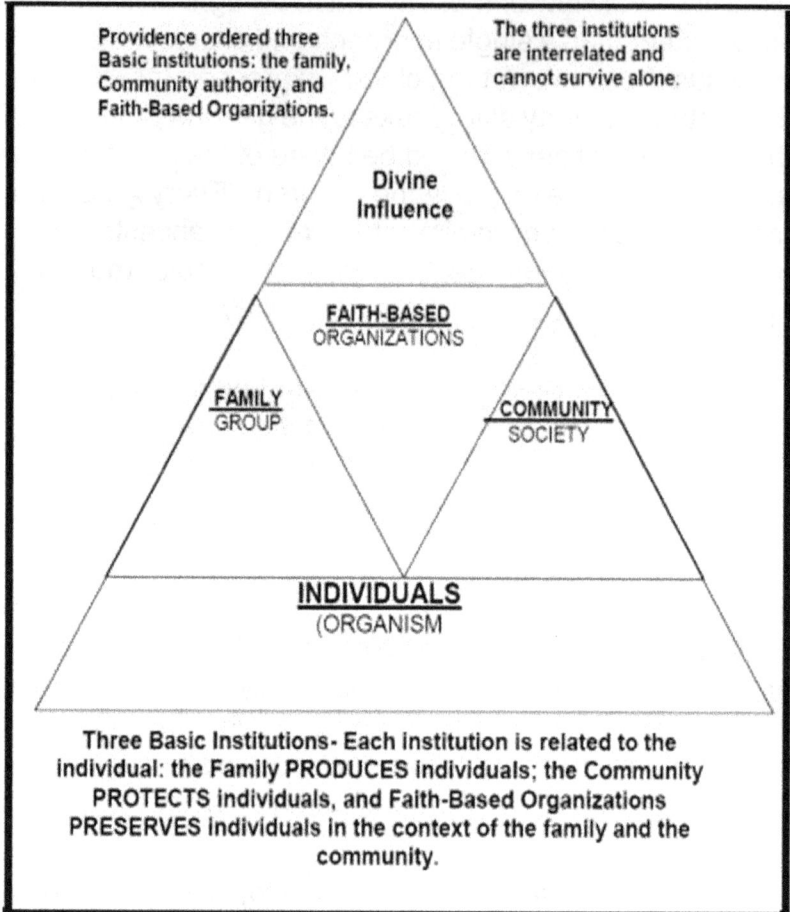

Providence ordered three Basic institutions: the family, Community authority, and Faith-Based Organizations.

The three institutions are interrelated and cannot survive alone.

Divine
Influence

FAITH-BASED
ORGANIZATIONS

FAMILY
GROUP

COMMUNITY
SOCIETY

INDIVIDUALS
(ORGANISM

Three Basic Institutions- Each institution is related to the individual: the Family PRODUCES individuals; the Community PROTECTS individuals, and Faith-Based Organizations PRESERVES individuals in the context of the family and the community.

Figure 2

These three primary entities are interrelated and cannot survive alone

Understanding how children functioned in their previous environment is a precondition to creating an atmosphere conducive to remedial and surrogate parenting. A philosophy of life begins with an awareness of three basic institutions that were intended and structured by Divine Providence for the benefit of children. They are the **nuclear family**, **formally constituted community**, and

faith-based entities. These three primary entities are interrelated and cannot survive alone. Providence designed the physical makeup of human beings so that individuals would be **produced** within an established nuclear family, **protected** in a formally, constituted community, and **preserved** in the context of both family and community through the influence of a faith-based entity.

Custodial caregivers must clearly comprehend that the primary concern of Providence in establishing these basic institutions was the welfare of individuals. When concern for children's rights and justice is placed on the back burner in order to increase the free-time of dysfunctional parents, the process of childcare is in danger. In a custodial environment a child must never become just a number to be discarded or dealt with arbitrarily. Of course, there are times when a child's behavior violates rules and custodial culture and eliminates them from productive involvement. In such case, the entity must function for the good of the whole.

The nuclear family is a basic social unit consisting of parents and their children living in one household and connected to an extended family. Now families are scattered all over the world seeking relief, recreation, and retirement. When children are born without the care and nurture of a loving two-parent family and grow up in an immoral and indifferent community without the influence of a faith-based entity, many problems are inflicted on society because of dysfunctional and defiled children. These difficulties complicate the work of custodial care.

A formally constituted community is a group of people gathered in a neighborhood and linked by similarity, kinship, and identity. Within the pluralistic society, neighborhoods are mixed, ethnic groups intermarry, children are born out of wedlock, and some are left abandoned, neglected or abused without parental guidance or support.

It has become difficult for the extended family to care for all the unsupported children whose carefree, sick, or overwhelmed parents have gone their own way and left the responsibility to grandparents or others.

In the effort to protect individuals, the community often protects the guilty from the wrath of others. Yet, the community is structured to punish individuals who violate the conventional wisdom and community authority but does little or nothing to correct the dysfunctional family unit that neglects or abuses the children. Why are those who abandon children not punished to the fullest extent of the law? Why are parents not required to financially support their children or pay for the support others must provide? Society must consider both the protection of the child and the separation of those individuals who would harm the family and the children. Some are dismissive of the community and snub their nose at a moral society, but little is done to correct the problem. Why must a few pick up the broken children and pay the bill for their support and care?

A Faith-based Entity is a group of kindred souls identified by common beliefs and moral structure. The mobility of society and the immorality of the people have jeopardized the influence of faith-based organizations. All of this leaves the children bearing the burden of family dysfunction, community breakdown, and society's failures due to the lack of faith-based moral leadership and honorable elected leadership.

By default, some individuals, a few socially responsible companies, and faith-based entities have established bridges of hope for the children and are gathering the abandoned and abused into villages for remedial and surrogate parenting. This is an expensive endeavor with only a few bearing the cost of services rendered. The children's villages are filled with low-paid but dedicated staff that make a difference, but much more is needed.

A Cultural View of the World

When faith-based entities fail to reach a community with the message of social ethics and morality, children and families become dysfunctional. Practitioners and professionals may succeed with basic assistance that produces social services for the children, but this is a stop-gap measure. Individuals are limited in what they can do to solve the systemic problem of abandoned, neglected and abused children. In addition to community leaders, members of the social professions are confronted daily with the dysfunctional fallout of broken families, broken laws, and broken promises. Yet community leaders and the social professions have an opportunity for a contextual understanding of the secular market place often lost to faith-based leaders. In the past, an application of the essential elements of morality and fairness was left to clergy, academics, judiciary, and law enforcement who have limited contact and little understanding of the realities of the complex community and the dysfunctional families that produced the needy children. There remains a great fixed gulf between the moral convictions and the constructive community agenda. Sadly, the core values and moral fiber of the community have diminished and created a contextual atmosphere that breeds discrimination, segregation and a lack of justice or fairness for the children.

Why do morality and ethics have difficulty in a multi-cultural society? Why are children the primary victims of broken promises, broken laws, and broken families? What is the inferior process that weakens the moral fiber? Why has the faith-based message of grace and forgiveness failed to be a viable expression of morality to the community? To integrate basic moral values into a pluralistic community, individuals and groups must have a comprehensive grasp of the many aspects of culture and tradition and face them with an open mind and a willing heart. Priority must be given to the welfare of the children; then the community can begin to fix the problems that produced the needy children.

Why has caring for the children failed? Parents are to dwell together in harmony so their prayers would not be hindered. Partners in marriage are obligated to separate each other from participation in the immorality of the community lest their children become defiled. Yet, all individuals are responsible to a higher authority to conduct their life in keeping with stated moral and ethical standards. When these standards are broken everyone suffers, but the children endure the most hardships and long-term difficulties.

A Mixing Bowl of Culture and Tradition

Families and communities in a multicultural society are a mixing bowl of various cultures and traditions. Each person in the community has both the opportunity and obligation to live a just and honorable life, to care for the family and the children, and support organized structures that protect and defend the people. Each opening for constructive change requires personal action. There are occasions in most communities to produce positive change and moral progress; therefore, it becomes an obligation for all concerned to work toward such progress and transformation of their community. This is particularly the obligation of those individuals who are aware of the needs of abandoned, neglected, and abused children. If the children are not protected and preserved, the multicultural mixing bowl will become a simmering stew pot of festering frustration. Then, not only will the children be beaten down; civil society itself will go down the sewer drain to total debauchery from which there is no return.

Catalyst or Change Agent

A failure to understand the basic difference in children is much the same as confusing a catalyst and a change agent. Both have the same objective – producing change, but one is not changed in the process. There can be no true change in the children unless those precipitating the change are also changed as part of the ongoing progression. It must be an interactive process. Any failure to understand the difference between a catalyst and a functioning change agent has frustrated child caregivers for decades. A catalyst is not changed in the process of creating the course of action that brings about change in a child; a change agent is altered by the course of action itself and becomes a different functioning element. When caregivers begin to alter and change their attitude and behavior, the child will more readily see the need to make changes. It is this reciprocal or mutually responsive process that makes care giving work.

Surrogate Caregivers Concerns

Surrogate caregivers are concerned with the assessed levels of bonding, personality, knowledge base, character, and spiritual formations as they deal with the children. As new children come into a custodial facility, there is a time-lag in adjusting to the new environment. Caregivers must be sensitive to this observable occurrence. One may appropriately translate the early adjustment time frame of months into years in an application to growth and development of an individual child.

A child has a period of socialization during the first 6 months of life in which they develop a relationship with authority. During the next 6 months the child develops a sense of expectation from the environment. At about one year, the child begins to develop the beginnings of autonomy: walking, talking freely and thinking positively about the environment. This growth and development process continues and the progress should be recognized. As a child reaches early age and goes outside the facility for class, it takes about 6 months to learn the rules and develop relationships with new teachers. This is called socialization. During the next 6 months the child develops a sense of empathy in relationship with peers, adults, and teachers and is taught the meaning of justice and the expectations of their surroundings.

Most of the problems in children's behavior could be corrected at this stage if caregivers and teachers operated through tough love to adjust attitudes and behavior. Much of the funds spent on the courts and prisons could be diverted to improving the conditions for the children. When a child reaches a certain stage of autonomy at about age 13, it is much harder to make the necessary corrections.

Confidence is a Factor

Remedial development and growth begin with confidence. There must be confidence in the custodial care provided, confidence in the program and process the facility has as a priority, and also have confidence in the personnel and staff with whom one works. Without confidence in these categories, no custodial care facility or childcare program can function effectively regardless of the quality or quantity of personnel and funding. These factors must be considered in the remedial and surrogate parenting of needy children.

Understanding how children function in the context of the basic institutions is important to childcare and development. Age, background and experience have dissimilar impact on different individuals. All children are not equal and must be considered as individuals with both age-level maturity, background, positive and negative experience and personal and emotional feelings. To ignore these aspects is to fail as caregiver for children.

Caregiving is Situational

What may be good care for one child at a particular stage of development may not be good care for another child or even for the same child at a different developmental stage. Good care does two things: it matches the child's stage of development, and it empowers the child to progress toward self-direction. Good care is situational, yet it provides the long-term development of the child.

The entire custodial system is based on a growth and development from high structure to little or no structure, from kindergarten to work in which the structure or task is lessened and the relationship between caregiver and child grows systematically less until the child matures and is able to leave custodial care and make it in the workplace.

Quality and Quantity

Quality and quantity are mutually exclusive; increase one and decrease the other. There must be a proportional balance between these two elements to maintain stable growth and development. There is a limit to what one caregiver can do. If the staff is short-handed or unskilled, all the children undergo some unpleasantness and suffer personal loss. Perfection is not the goal of custodial care; growth and age-specific development is the true objective. Quality in childcare comes when children have a guide, coach, counselor, and friend who provide the freedom to search and learn and discover the way forward. Discovery is real learning and should be rewarded with marks of quality and words of praise.

Dual-Track Plan

In most custodial care facilities, children interface the process of remedial development in stages and may not consider the next step. In such cases, children cannot plan their life or career until the final stage is completed. Being unable to consider the next step may be acceptable for the very young in the early stages of elementary and primary school, but a lack of final stage planning cannot be considered adequate for those reaching their teen years. To take advantage of the stage evaluation process as well as providing children an overview of the process with guidance toward ultimate goals, some caregivers may consider a Dual-Track Plan (CPM-PERT).

Critical Path Method (CPM)

The Critical Path Method works backward from a perception of where the child should be at the time of leaving custodial care. CPM is used in construction when a builder views both an architect drawing of a completed building and a set of working drawings of how the building is to be constructed. The builder, with a clear view of both plans and a conception of the finished product, establishes target dates for each stage of development. The objective is to prepare the child for the real world after they leave custodial care.

Working back from the target date, the builder considers time, material, and contingencies to establish a construction schedule. At this point the builder must start at the beginning, structure the building in stages, and arrange for an evaluation process based on the architect's plans. Each aspect of the construction must be done in sequence with the timeline affected by the duration of each stage. With the CPM the builder may evaluate progress using a Performance Evaluation Review Technique (PERT). To do this, the caregiver must understand clearly the age-specific level of development of each child. Age or physical size is not sufficient criteria to judge progress because each child is different.

Performance Evaluation Review Technique (PERT)

Each aspect of a project is viewed in the light of prerequisites. As each stage is satisfactorily completed, the project moves to the subsequent stage until the project is completed. Without the Critical Path Method timeline, the performance evaluation review technique cannot remain on schedule. It takes viewing the child development from both the beginning and the end with the sequence of stages to complete the preparation for the child to leave custodial care. This must be done without loss or waste of time. The clock is running on each child. Certain things must be done within specific timeframes or the opportunity passes and may never return. This requires lots of planning and preparation by the caregiver.

Planning Cycle of Custodial Care

There are three reasons for planning in custodial child care. First, custodial leadership and staff must (1) **plan for the future**. Unless this is done one cannot fulfill the second reason for planning to (2) **take advantage of opportunities**. When caregivers and staff understand the purpose, know the objectives, value the goals, and are clear on the standards by which progress will be measured, they can take advantage of each opportunity to advance the real agenda of development and prepare the child for the real world. Only then should caregivers and staff take time to (3) **deal with problems**. Many problems are solved through using the opportunities that circumstance presents. Time is a great healer of a troubled soul. As the inner spirit heals, the child's behavior will improve. Caregivers must be kind and gentle, remember some of the children have been physically abused by adults and have keen memories of the harsh speech and acts. Progress in the behavior area can usually be accomplished by asking questions: What can be done better for this child? What can be done differently for this child? What can be done new for this child? How is this child progressing in relationship to age-specific goals and expectations?

In order to achieve motility or the demonstration of movement by independent means, there must be purposeful action not just activity or busyness, there must be a planning process. When custodial caregivers are sure of where they are going and clear of what they are attempting

to do, the best methods can be used to complete the process. When this is done adequately in a timely manner
the process will achieve satisfactory results. This can only
be done if the choice of methodology is a result of a planning process.

Planning Process

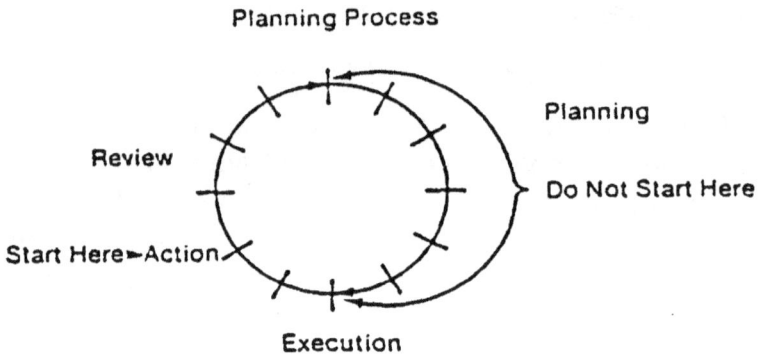

Figure 3

The planning and review Process

Finally, after custodial caregivers and staff have used
each opportunity to facilitate progress toward the stated
objectives for custodial care, the child must be prepared
for entry into the real world of work and responsibility.
Once this is done there will be time for solving the remaining problems. Each problem becomes a learning experience for both the child and the caregiver.

Children should not be blamed for problems that were
caused by their previous environment or other people; the
program and process of custodial care must be examined
and evaluated first and corrections made to any inferior
aspect of the process. Once an analysis of difficulties is
made, caregivers and staff can begin constructing a superior process to advance custodial care of children. This
planning process will result in a revision of both methods
and policy.

Policy is answers worked out in advance for antici- pated questions. Methodology includes the approach one takes to answer all unanswered questions and the course of action required to move custodial care toward the stated goals. Caregivers and staff must remember that one may not construct a superior process until the inferior process has been corrected. This includes the child, the caregiver, and the custodial process. The proper order: correct the inferior then construct the superior. There is always room for improvement.

A policy is answers worked out in advance of anticipated questions.

Figure 4

The planning cycle depends on time, relationship and individual maturity. The caregiver must adjust to the matu- rity level of the child to accomplish the developmental pro- cess. The process is simple: First, it is a **telling** activity that requires high task, but low relationship. This leads to the necessity to **sell** the process to the child and requires both high task and high relationship. In the next stage the caregiver's behavior becomes **participating** through high relationship/low task to excite and direct the self-activity of the child. Finally, as the child matures, the caregiver may **delegate** certain activities and parts of the discussion ses- sion to the child. At times such delegated aspects of the discussion will be related directly to the child and indirectly to the custodial institution. It should be "One for all and all for one."

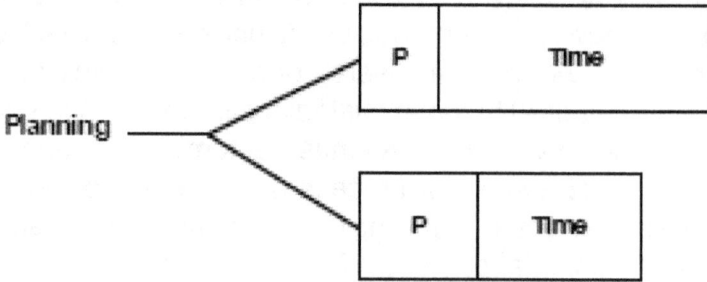

Figure 5

The simple goals of the surrogate childcare process are:

 1) Stimulate the interest of the child,

 2) Arouse their spirit of inquiry, and

 3) Get the child talking and otherwise involved.

The caregiver must excite and direct the self-activity of the child, and as a rule do nothing for them that they can do for themselves. Children in custodial care must be taught self-reliance and to do for themselves all things for which they are capable. Growth and development is in fact the process of action and discovery.

Like footprints each child is different!

CHAPTER THREE

PRINCIPLES OF REMEDIAL PARENTING

The First Rule of Surrogate Parenting

This first rule of surrogate parenting relates to the Small Ball Theory that suggests that most caregivers in remedial and surrogate parenting overdo the effort to push the child into progress. In parenting there is a guideline that comes from agriculture, the law of diminishing returns. It seems there is only so much that one can do in the effort to make a plant grow and beyond that point the effort becomes harmful or negative. In other words, there is a point when more is too much. Growth is gradual and cannot be rushed.

The Small Ball Theory is simple. If one pushes too hard or tries to do too much, actual progress will slow, and, if the effort is continued to force growth, eventually the whole developmental process could be jeopardized. The first rule then is to take it slow and easy. Children are delicate, especially abandoned, neglected, or abused children. Growth is slow and incremental, but it is also a deliberate and intentional process over time. Use a small ball!

The Small Ball Theory

The illustration below is of a man, but you can mentally put a child in the seat. Use a little imagination. The small ball theory suggests that custodial caregivers overdo the effort to motivate a child to grow and develop. They use too many big words, too many grand projects without sizing the ball to the child and the problem. All healthy growth is slow and incremental. Rapid growth is considered cancerous or abnormal. Let the child grow; do not try to force the child to grow. This will discombobulate (there is a big word) the child; it means to confuse or bring discomfort to somebody.

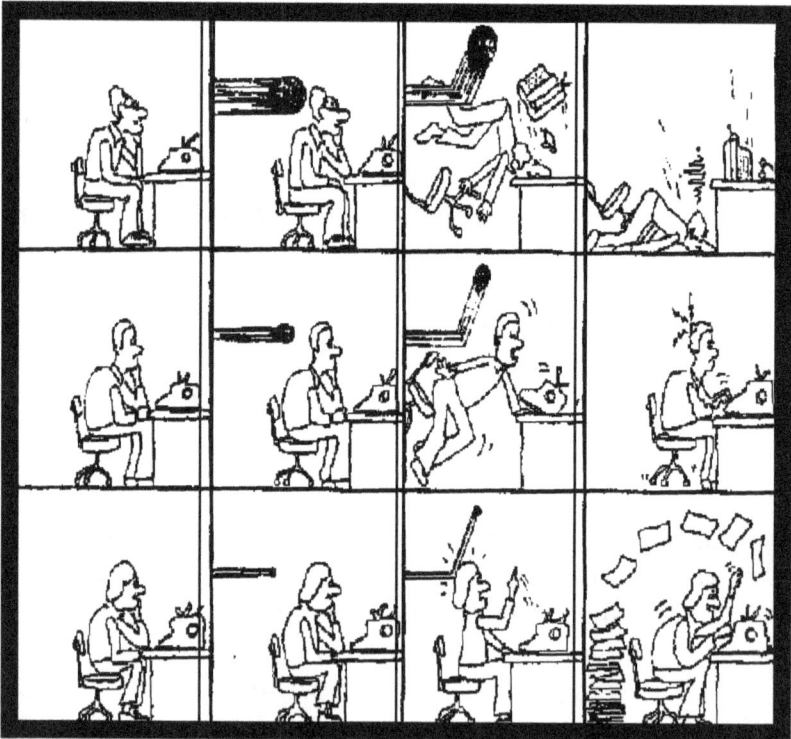

Figure 6

Remedial and Surrogate Parenting

Principles in childrearing are based on the standard practices of parenting that come natural to most birth parents; however, every female and male adult has both maternal and paternal instincts. This means they have some inborn knowledge and skills that enable them to care for a child. Just think: for centuries before psychologists, modern medicine, or professional childcare specialists, young girls and old women were raising the leaders of the world. This they did with natural ability and Godgiven wisdom and patience.

A child is a child is a child...regardless of who the birth parents were, a child in one's presence should be considered with all the maternal and paternal affection and discipline that one could muster. One does not need to be a licensed professional, a trained medical person, a special child psychologist, or a near relative to care for a child. Although this has been the responsibility of parents, extended family, and relatives throughout history, and grandma and Aunt Susie did a fairly good job in raising Johnny and Jane when they were left without proper care. The point here is caregivers do not have to be a member of the family, a professional or credentialed person to love and care for a disadvantaged child. In fact, some of the wealthiest families in the world hire young girls and mature women as nannies and they perform the task of surrogate parenting well. This means if caregivers use the common sense and maternal and paternal instincts that are naturally a part of their make-up, they can do well in exercising the skills of parenting. Remember, Benjamin Spock's (1903-1998) message to caregivers was simple and straight forward: "You know more than you think you do."

Parenting includes the experiences, skills, qualities, and responsibilities involved in being a legal guardian and in teaching and/or caring for a child. When normal parenting is interrupted by death, sickness, or abandonment, a child must have continued nurturing and care. This is where the concept of surrogate parenting enters the custodial arena. When one takes the place of another as a substitute or replacement, they become the surrogate parent. To care for a child is a noble task.

Remedial parenting is simply recognizing that a child has a problem based on neglect or oversight and acting to remedy or solve the problem by engaging in affectionate and disciplined care-giving. Well-meaning parents, unknowingly neglect parts of a child's upbringing. When a child is sick or for some reason misses a day at school when a vital step in the learning process is covered, the child may always be mentally challenged in a particular area unless a surrogate parent/tutor does the remedial work to replace the missing information. This is also clear in the behavioral difficulties. Some parents are just unable to adequately and constructively discipline the child and the bad behavior persists until a surrogate parent/teacher deals directly with the problem. Acting to improve a child's behavior is a worthy task and although it may be unappreciated, the process has enormous benefits for the child in the long term.

Childcare is a Flower Garden

Parenting is similar to growing a flower garden. The process requires multiple steps and if a step were neglected the results would be evident in the harvest for all to see. Buying cut flowers from the local flower shop and tying the blooms on dead stems in the backyard garden would be a waste of energy and funds. If someone hired an expensive professional to "counsel or tutor" a child who was undisciplined or simply missed some earlier instruction or guidance in school, it could be equally as wasteful. What most children need is someone with common sense and lots of love and patience to search out the problem and provide a simple and practical solution.

Childcare and growing a flower garden have many similarities. First, they require diligent cultivation of the soil. This is hard work, meticulous work, and is often painstaking. Nurturing a flower to grow is a rewarding endeavor, but the benefit is delayed. Before the bloom of achievement comes, there must be careful, prayerful planting. This must be matched with unceasing effort that includes struggle and a little sweat. Childcare is a full-time endeavor. When one is not directly involved, the time must be used in thinking and planning the next step in the process. The constant attention is matched only by saintly patience born out of endurance, persistence and courage. There will be weeds, draught, pestilences, and unseen problems that plague a garden of flowers or the life of a growing child. Then after all the physical, mental, and spiritual energy, the garden and the child must be touched by the hand of divine providence. Sorrow may endure for the night, but joy comes in the morning.

An example of remedial work

Early in my teaching career I tutored children who were failing. I did this as a community service without charge because I knew how a child could miss one small aspect of a lesson and be functionally handicapped the balance of their life. One day a mother brought a small boy from kindergarten for assistance with counting. It seems the teacher would not pass him to the first grade because he could not count to 100. I asked the child a few simple questions to establish rapport and then asked him to count.

He quickly counted: 1, 2, 3, 4, 5, 6, 7, 8, 9, 10, 11,12, 13,14,15,16,17,18,19, 20, and stopped. I asked, "Can you count to 100?" He said, "10, 20, 30, 40, 50, 60, 70, 80,

90, 100!" I asked the mother, what is the problem? Her response, "The teacher said he couldn't count to 100."

He counted again 1 to 20 and I encouraged him to continue, He counted, "2011, 2012, 2013, etc". I pointed to 30 and asked that he count," 30, 3011, 3012, 3013, etc". I asked the mother if he had been sick and missed any school days. The answer was that he missed nearly two weeks early in the year. I had my answer. He had missed the simple lesson that demonstrated that at 20 the counter replaces the "0" with 1 – 9 just as if counting 1 to 10. I showed him the process and asked him to count. 20, 21, 22, etc.

He counted, "20, 2011, 2012, (I conked him lightly on the head with a yellow pencil to get his attention); the mother stood up. I asked her to be seated saying this is a free lesson and your child will be fixed in three minutes. I raised my pencil in the air and asked the boy to count: He counted 1 to 20 easily and hesitated. I raised my pencil to keep him focused, he continued…20 elev…21, 22, 23, etc. The problem was fixed. There was nothing wrong with the child. He had simply missed a small part of the instruction.

It was that simple. All he needed was an adult to take the time to fill in the blank in a missed lesson. That was remedial instruction or remedial parenting. Most children need it. All children in custodial care must have it. Just use common sense. You can do it!

My mother was a school teacher in her younger years and later the dean of a nursing school and dean of women at a college. She shared with me two experiences that are appropriate to remedial and surrogate parenting:

The One-Room Grammar School Experience

Early on, mother taught in a rural grammar school where grades 1 – 8 met in the same room. She explained how the dynamics worked to the advantage of education for all the children. When a slow learner did not exactly understand the third grade math lesson, they would have a chance to listen again when the lesson was given to the next third grade class. Being one year older, the lesson was better understood. Likewise, a bright or advanced fifth grade student ahead of his class in math could listen to the sixth or seventh grade math lesson and continue advancing without becoming bored. Another factor that mother pointed out was that as the brightest students reached the top two levels of the school, the future teachers and most promising mothers-to-be began assisting the younger children with their lessons. In this case, everyone was a winner. The young received the needed assistance and the older students gained experience in helping others. Custodial care can have some of the same advantages when the advance learners and older residents assist the caregivers with the younger children's lessons and behavior. If a child needs special tutoring in a given subject, pair that child with an older student who is good in the subject. The experience will benefit both and will advance the whole cause of development.

The System Declared the Boy Retarded

In the city school system, a young boy was declared to be limited in learning capacity or retarded. The mother, although only a high school graduate, told the teachers they were wrong that her child was bright and they just did not take the time to properly teach him. She took him out of public school and home schooled the boy through the 12th grade level and he was admitted by examination to a state university. He graduated with high honors and the university gave him a place in the graduate program. He completed the graduate degree course at the top of his class. So much for what the system knew and when they knew it! And so much for what maternal love and patience can do when a child is loved and understood.

Remedial and surrogate caregivers have many opportunities to bring the bright light of achievement to the countenance of a child. Do not miss this opportunity. Opportunity equals obligation. Life goes forward and an opportunity passed is an opportunity that is lost! Time does not go backwards!

Guidelines for Surrogate Caregivers

There are rules and guidelines to enable surrogate caregivers to be effective in childcare in spite of the previous difficulties a child may have experienced. All children in custodial care need special attention, but mostly they need affection and tough love. What is meant by tough love? It is a caring but strict attitude adopted toward a child with a problem as distinct from an attitude of indulgence. When a child has been neglected or permitted to behave badly without consequences, a predisposition develops that breeds abnormal behavior and generally a negative attitude toward all authority including caregivers and teachers. Therefore, it is vital that a caregiver have full knowledge of the child's previous environment and the last living arrangements, including where the child slept. A caregiver needs to know if the child had a baby sitter, what was the sitter's age and how much time did they spend with the child alone.

The child's present physical and emotional health, together with the general aspects of personality and their knowledge base will determine when, where, and how much attention the caregiver must devote to a particular child. All these factors determine the child's ability and willingness to listen or attend with interest to the caregiver. It is the responsibility of the caregiver to obtain and maintain the attention of the child. A good rule of thumb is that a child's attention span is roughly tied to age: a caregiver may keep the attention of a two-year old for two minutes and then they must do something to reconnect with the child. On the same scale, a four-year old has an attention span of about four minutes, six-year old about six minutes, etc. With this knowledge the caregiver must stimulate interest, arouse a spirit of inquiry, and get the child involved in the process to make progress with any aspect of growth and development.

Caregivers must always use language (words) and tone (the way one speaks is an indicator of what they are feeling or thinking) that the child accepts and understands. The caregiver must know what the child already knows on the subject at hand so they can build a bridge over the fixed gap of "not knowing" to the new things the child is to learn. Simply stated, a child learns by going from the known to the unknown. The facts must always be age-specific and related to the reality of the child. The caregiver must start with what the child knows and proceed to new things. The caregiver must enable the child to process the content of a conversation or lesson by permitting them to learn by discovery. The caregiver must use a minimum of telling, a great deal of selling, total involvement and participation, and some delegating to keep the child interested and excited about learning.

Remedial learning requires the caregiver to be certain the child hears exactly what is said and understands the meaning of all words spoken. If the child is able to repeat in his/her own words what was said, they probably understand. When a child is able to give an example or illustration of what was said, it becomes clear they understand. The ability to use the information given is the goal of the interaction. The child acquires knowledge by using information and facts in answering a question or solving a problem. This moves the data from the short-term memory to the long-term memory or into the knowledge base.

When a child does not clearly understand instructions or correction, they cannot be responsible for following it.

Caregivers must be certain that children clearly understand what is said and meant before the child is reprimanded or punished for "not doing what they were told." Most children in custodial care have had sufficient criticism and scolding.

One-third of all the caregivers face-to-face time with a child must be used in review and application to be certain the child understood what was said or taught. Repeat until you are certain the child has a clear grasp of the subject at hand. Provide illustrations and examples of expected behavior or action. Children enjoy pleasing adults and caregivers and gain good self-esteem when they are able to understand and act properly.

How does a caregiver talk to a child? Regardless of the schedule with groups and classes, the caregiver must spend some quality time talking directly with a child. Pick a time when meaningful eye contact can be established. The chat does not have to be heavy or even focused, but should follow some simple plan. The caregiver should watch the child's eye movements during any conversation. Caregivers must become aware of facial expressions and eye motion between something that is stressful or mean-ingless to the child. Watch for excitement, enthusiasm, in-terest, discomfort, irritation or even anger. There will most likely be a full range of emotions, the caregiver should learn the triggers that change the body language and both positive and negative reactions of the child.

Ask age-specific questions about what the child did today or the day before. Use a little common sense and discuss things that happened that are on the child's mind. Ask about people in the child's life and permit a search for some good memories. Be cautious when asking about their previous environment; just include questions about the past as a matter of course and do not make a big deal of past difficulties. Be certain the child knows that past dif-ficulties were caused by others.

Caregivers may gradually increase limitations and boundaries on activities that are negative or harmful and that involve others. If a child is having difficulty with another person in the facility or at school, they will be uncomfortable dealing with a caregiver about the matter and will attempt to avoid a discussion. If it is a problem in the facility, deal with it directly. If it is an outside problem (at school or from visiting relatives) find out where these people live and look for an opportunity to speak directly to the parents of a child or directly to an adult involved. When you are present, it will be much easier to flush out problems. A big part of the problem is solved by the other people knowing that you know about the incident.

Self-Directed Caregivers

Parents and all caregivers ought to move toward becoming self-directed learners themselves. They must believe in its importance, have a trust in human beings, and maintain an open attitude as well as an understanding of opportunity that the self-directed model affords. Caregivers need to be aware of the characteristics of a self-directed person but still work within the rules and regulations of custodial care. Rarely do parents get a second chance to bring up a child. Occasionally, Providence brings children back into the care of biological parents. When this happens, these parents may benefit by studying the seven characteristics of caregivers below:

1. **Self-acceptance**. Caregivers who have self-awareness have a "can do" attitude and a positive valuing of the self as an entity worthy of improvement.

2. **Planning.** Caregivers who plan are able to diagnose their personal needs, set appropriate goals in the light of those needs, and devise effective strategies for achieving the goals. Such caregivers willingly make use of the assistance and advice of others.

3. **Intrinsic motivation.** Caregivers are intrinsically motivated individuals and persist in learning activities without external controls in the form of rewards or sanctions. They are also likely to continue learning outside formal programs offered by the facility and to delay or even forgo competing gratification in order to proceed with personal development in the custodial field.

4. **Internalized evaluations**. Self-directed caregivers are able to act as their own evaluation agents, giving accurate estimates of the quality of their own performance based on evidence they collect themselves. They normally will accept external evaluation as valid only when the qualifications of the reviewer are established independently of social role and when the evaluation agrees with their own evidence.

5. **Openness to experience**. Caregivers who are open to experience engage in new kinds of activities that result in growth and personal progress. Curiosity, tolerance of ambiguity, preference, complexity and even playfulness represent motives for entering into new activities and imply openness to experience.

6. **Flexibility.** Caregivers who have flexibility in life and work imply a willingness to change goals or styles and to use exploratory, trial-and-error approaches to problem solving. Here, failure is countered with adaptive behavior rather than by denial or withdrawal

7. **Autonomy.** Autonomous caregivers choose to engage in types of activities that may not be seen as important within a particular cultural context. Such individuals are able to question the normative standards of a given time and place as to what kinds of activity and experiences are valuable and permissible. In other words, they are mature people who have a good self-image.

Like footprints each child is different!

CHAPTER FOUR

LISTENING AND REMEDIAL DEVELOPMENT

The Language of the Heart

Individuals who feel an urge, desire, or call to work with children especially those who want to work with abandoned, neglected, and abused children must learn to speak the language of the heart. Note that h-**ear**-t contains an "ear" - this is the "ear" of the heart with which one listens attentively to the words of children. A plaque in my home reads: "Called to listen to the needs of others, even those unspoken." This is a good maxim for a caregiver of children because a child has many "unspoken words" that a caregiver must listen for and understand.

Dynamic Listening

A parent or surrogate caregiver must work through the maze and get to the heart of the child. Being involved in dynamic listening to the children under care is a big step in that direction. Dynamic listening is active, vigorous, energetic, and is always focused on the child. Dynamic listening encourages both the caregiver and the child to listen with attention and stick to the task at hand in spite of all distractions. Listening is an important skill for all caregivers who, as a rule, tend to talk too much. The caregiver should consider themselves to be a tutor whose goal is to allow the child to learn by discussion. When tutors are dynamic listeners, it encourages the child to become an active learner. Giving a child full attention is difficult but it is a mark of a good tutor and caregiver. Time is limited and caregivers often demonstrate impatience with a child who is slow to grasp an idea or concept, but spending time in dynamic listening with a child will result in quality childcare and in a quantity learning experience.

Listening is the Key to Understanding

The issue is not hearing, but listening. Three levels of hearing relate to human communication. The first level is the level of non-hearing, "having ears and hear not;" in other words, the ear hears the sound but ignores it. An example would be a ticking clock that is ignored until someone asks for the time. A second level of hearing is the ability to hear the words, record them in a special part of the brain and even recall the exact words but never obtaining the understanding of their meaning. This is a kind of recording/playback device that is often used to avoid the content of the conversation. The final level is listening. This requires both analysis and action. When one gives attention to the spoken word, listens to the sounds, and understands the meaning, this is listening. This requires one to examine the words in detail in order to better understand or draw conclusions. When such an analysis takes place, normally some kind of action or response is forthcoming. Listening by both the caregiver and the child is necessary for progress in remedial development.

Listening says, "Come closer, touch my heart and mind, but not by body." It has been noted that "listening is the highest form of touching absent physical contact."

Listening has also been associated with a replacement for sexual intimacy. This may explain the behavior of some adults who care for a child, and may even "love" the child, but do not know how to properly listen and show their affection without some kind of selfish sexual contact. This may explain the root of sexual abuse by family members, but it is not to excuse such behavior. This is just an effort to come to an understanding as to how such behavior could be perpetrated on a helpless child by someone who is supposed to have natural affection for the child. When sexual or physical abuse has occurred by a family member in the past environment, the custodial care process is more complicated.

The surrogate caregiver must consider this in close dealings with the child. Normally, no touching of the child unless it is initiated by the child. A child has vivid memories of previous encounters with adults that began with "touching;" consequently, an innocent touch by the caregiver may trigger a frightening recall of a terrifying experience. Such an episode could reset the child's behavior to the negative condition that brought them to custodial care. The caregiver and the child could be back to square one and a new caregiver may be required.

When children feel the caregiver is listening to them, they will be more apt to attend with interest to what the caregiver is saying. In other words, they will also listen. This long moving line of events and episodes runs in installments in both directions! Remedial child development is a process not an event. Real communication requires listening and receiving on the part of both the caregiver and the child, but the burden to assure the listening is placed on the adult. It is not an easy task to be a caregiver to a needy or neglected child; if the child has been physically or sexually abused it is more problematic. If caregivers follow the rules such a complication can usually be avoided; however, some children may deliberately fake such an encounter to get special attention or to force a change in their custodial caregiver. Normally, a child should be believed in case of any accusation, but the caregiver has rights also. Supervising staff must consider the rights of both in dealing with any charge of mistreatment or change in personnel.

The Four C's of Listening

Do not confuse hearing and listening. Hearing is the physical aspect of perceiving sound. Listening is analyzing and understanding the sound---it is hearing with a purpose. Primary listening includes basic skills: concentration, consideration, contemplation, and comportment. These are called the four-C's of listening.

1. **Concentration** permits one to be attentive to the words being spoken and become absorbed in the meaning of the words. This enables immediate thinking of how to apply and relate the meaning to the general discussion.

2. **Consideration** is to add value to the words heard, reflect on this value by reproducing the concepts in one's own words, and deliberately attributing value to the child because of the meaning of the words.

3. **Contemplation** is mulling over the significance of the words and the worth, importance, and usefulness of the discussion.

4. **Comportment** is the overall behavior of the listener and a general assessment that answers the question: "Do the child's words match the conduct and character exhibited?" This is the final effort to add credibility to the discussion. The more the listener values the speaker, the greater the significance of the words spoken. When a child's words are valued, listening is both easy and rewarding. The listener must separate fantasy from fact when children are telling stories about their previous environment. Remember, children have a great imagination and often conjure up fantasy playmates and fabricate stories. Although the stories are based on

events, they may be remembered in a way the child dealt with the episode in order to cope with the situation. Dynamic listening by the caregiver must engage the child sufficiently to understand what part is fact and what is a flight of the imagination.

Poor Listeners

Most parents and surrogate caregivers tend to be poor listeners. How well a caregiver listens is a major factor in effectiveness with children. A caregiver listens to obtain information, to better understand the child, and to learn important facts not yet in evidence that can come only from the memory and recall of the child. Clearly the improvement of listening skills should be a regular goal of custodial care staff and caregivers. Everyone, including the children, will benefit when listening skills are improved. Good listening skills will also prevent conflict and misunderstandings among the staff that children in custodial care are "street smart" to sense such disagreements.

Listening Strategies

Maintain eye contact with the child when he/she is speaking. Face-to-face contact keeps one focused on the task at hand and keeps both parties involved. Focus on content by listening to every word. Forget about the faulty memory or halting speech; just concentrate on the words and their true meaning. Avoid personal or emotional reaction to anything said. At times one hears what they want to hear and not what is actually said. Remain objective and open-minded. Do not permit distractions to cause your mind to wander. Avoid anything that disturbs your concentration on what is being said. Make certain you are as comfortable as the location and situation permits. Listening is not a passive act. You must concentrate on what is said in order to process the information and use it for advantage for the child. Maintain an active role in the conversation or be a good silent listener if that is appropriate. Use any gap in the rate of speech to assimilate the words. Always keep focused on the child before you. Practice good listening skills and your listening will improve.

There are several ways to improve listening skills. Be deliberate with your listening and response and constantly remind yourself that your objective is to truly hear what the child is saying, even the unspoken stuff.

Attend with interest to what is being said. Give the child your undivided attention. Do not waste time; it is precious. Do not be distracted by thinking about a rebuttal when you should be listening, you will miss something important. Remember, the children are watching and listening in group settings do not permit yourself to have side conversations when you should be listening.

Demonstrate to others that you are listening. Smile and nod and use other facial expressions to let the child know you are listening. Small verbal comments such as yes, uh huh, may encourage the child to speak more frankly.

Offer constructive comments. Do not let your own assumptions or beliefs distort what is being said. Listeners are first required to understand what is being said. Disagreement or questions come later. When the opportunity is presented or there is a time for questions, be kind and paraphrase by saying, "What I heard…" "Did you say…?" "Is this what you mean…?"

Avoid premature conclusions. Do not interrupt when the children are speaking. It frustrates you and it totally irritates children because they think you are not listening just complaining. It is usually best to wait for a logical opening to express yourself.

Provide a measured response. If you know the facts to be wrong or the child expressed a lack of understanding of the data in the records, clarify the information for the child in a constructive tone. Be candid, open and honest in all responses.

A Failure to Listen

A failure to listen is insulting and equivalent to a social snub. Children are particularly susceptible to this feeling. When children sense that no one is listening, they feel defenseless and exposed to dangers seen and unseen. Listening then becomes a form of protection and a show of affection that is deeply appreciated by a child. Caregivers must practice dynamic listening with at-risk children. The caregiver may be tempted to divide their time between or among several children, but they must never divide their love, which is often perceived by a child as time with them – a kind of ministry of presence.

Always Multiply Love

Love is something caregivers must never divide; it ought to be multiplied by the number of children in their care circle. Love is understood as T-I-M-E! Since there are only 24 hours in a day and there is no way to expand the time, caregivers can multiply their time by grouping children with similar needs for a group session. It takes time to build a relationship with a child who has been abandoned, abused, or neglected. Caregivers must be willing to invest considerable time and multiply their affection to include all children under their care. There can be no favorites; however, some children have special needs and therefore need more time with the caregiver. Children are sensitive to being left out, overlooked, or neglected, especially children who have been negatively conditioned by their previous environment.

Rome was not built in a day and a neglected or abused child will not be restored to a normal developmental process in a few days. One rule of thumb is that it will take as long to correct a problem as it took to create the problem in the first place. Everyone wants things to move a little faster, but it may take as long to solve the problem as it did to create the malady in the first place. For example, if a child has survived in a negative environment for three years without sufficient bonding to a parent or guardian, it may take three years for a custodial caregiver to penetrate the inner child and develop the necessary bonding to make a real difference in the child's age-specific behavior and personal development. Consequently, the younger a child is when placed in custodial care the easier it is to emphasize the positive and eliminate the negative sufficiently to make a meaningful difference in behavior and development. Remedial work is time consuming and at times troubling for both the caregiver and the child. Therefore, patience is required.

What is patience? The Greeks named sick people waiting to see a physician, patients because they had to remain under the pressure of their illness until the physician could provide relief.   Patience is the ability to remain under the pressure of difficult circumstances until the restoration of normalcy occurs. One is patient with circumstances that cannot be easily changed and longsuffering with the individuals involved. What is longsuffering in childcare? It is love all stretched out over T-I-M-E that includes a good dose of "enduring patience" with circumstances that cannot be easily changed and "love all stretched out" in dealing with the child.

Surrogate Childcare is Climbing a Difficult Hill

Caring for children in the custodial arena is a difficult task. It is similar to climbing a long and difficult hill with lots of rough and dangerous places. It is also a fearful journey, because one does not know exactly what is just around the bend. Even though such a hill has been successfully traversed before, dealing with troubled and abused children always has unexpected dangers. Being a caregiver for children who are not yours by birth is filled with pitfalls and dangers, but the rewards are beyond measure. This reward comes not only in the faint first smile of a child or the joy of seeing the sparkle return to troubled eyes; it comes with the realization that if one saves a child they have saved a life and made one ready for parenting and a productive life in society. On top of all this, there is the blessing that comes from the Heavenly Father who faithfully rewards those who seek diligently to guide children along the straight and narrow path that leads to life eternal. As difficult as it may seem, remedial and surrogate parenting in the custodial arena can restore children to a safe and secure lifestyle that leads to a happy and productive life. John Bunyan's difficult struggle to serve others is a good example of spiritual achievement in a difficult environment.

Pilgrim's Progress

John Bunyan, an Englishman, wrote many books, but one stands out above all others; it was Pilgrim's Progress written in prison. Bunyan felt a call to serve others but refused to permit the English government or the Church of England to endorse his credentials. He felt that a call from God was sufficient authorization to serve. For this conviction of independence he served twelve years in prison in the Tower of London. During that period, with only a quill, ink, and paper, Bunyan wrote Pilgrim's Progress about the journey of Christian on his pilgrimage to heavenly heights. His book has out sold all other books in the English language with the exception of the English Bible.

In documenting the progress of a Christian pilgrim, Bunyan wrote a most fascinating story. In many respects Christian's pilgrimage parallels the custodial caregiver's struggle to bring about remedial development for abandoned and abused children. Such a venture is indeed "climbing the Hill of Difficulty." In Bunyan's story as Christian struggled up the Hill of Difficulty he met two frightened and nervous men running down hill. One was named Timorous and the other Fearful. As these nervous and frightened men passed, they yelled to Christian, "Don't go up there. There are lions up there!" Christian, without hesitation, responded, "To go back is nothing but death, I will go forward!" This is the attitude a surrogate caregiver must possess.

When Christian arrived at the top of the Hill of Difficulty, he saw that lions were indeed there but he noticed they were chained with a short chain and if he walked the "straight and narrow path" between them, the lions could not reach him. As he passed the lions he also noticed they were old, feeble, and their teeth were broken. He realized the "straight and narrow way" protected him from the intimidating lions. Remedial and surrogate caregivers should not be threatened by the pitfalls or dangers on the developmental journey with the child. They should approach the process with confidence. Perhaps a brief prayer once painted on a small stone could shed light on parenting or a remedial caregiver's positive attitude:

Lord help me to remember that nothing will happen to me today that you and I together can't handle!

A realistic word! Childcare in any environment is difficult, but rewarding. You may struggle, but the end result will be rewarding. To know that you did your best is also a reward of the first order! Certainly there are predatory lions along the way, but good programming and a little prayer will chain and restrain the "lions" so they cannot reach you personally. For the sake of the children, one must walk the straight path and persevere.

A word of caution! Should you fail in your struggle to adequately turn a child's life around, remember when you do your best...the rest is in God's hands. During the American Civil War, General Lee wrote his wife a letter explaining how the war had negatively impacted his future and obstructed some of his plans and that the interruption would leave him less time to accomplish certain goals. His wife wrote back a most telling response: "What you do not get done; God intends others to do!" This is good insight for the caregiver. Having done your best, God has someone else to take the next step and do the rest. At least the child will know that someone cared; and who knows just what part of your effort did take hold and will bring forth productive fruit in due season.

A surrogate care arena is a place of committed caregivers and volunteers who supply the remedial training needed to gain an age-specific level of development for children in need.

When designed to apply the medicine of laughter to the dry bones and broken spirit of children, surrogate childcare provides a happy place filled with the giggles and laughter of children at play.

Like footprints each child is different!

CHAPTER FIVE

SURROGATE CHILD SOCIALIZATION

Early Stage Development

Surrogate Socialization normally takes place during the first six months of entry into the formal childcare process, depending on the age and maturity of the child. This is the time needed to orient a child to take part in the social and functional activities or behave in a friendly way toward others and to gain the basic skills required to function adequately in a custodial environment. During the first 6 months after coming into a surrogate relationship, children learn the operative rules and develop relationships with the caregiver and other children with whom they are housed. They learn to function with the custodial culture during the first few months. **This is also true of new individuals coming into a surrogate relationship at any level.**

A sense of belonging and learning the expectations of peers and surrogate caregivers is developed over time. It can take up to 12 months to develop **Surrogate Empathy** or the ability to understand the circumstance of their custody and develop an identity compatible with the compassion and feelings of others. It is not easy to develop sympathy or compassion for someone else's feelings or difficulties when the child is hurting also. Facilitating this accomplishment is an early task of the caregiver.

Surrogate Care Autonomy for the staff may not be reached during the first year.   It normally takes at least one full year for new individuals to fit the concept of custodial care and the childcare culture into an autonomous lifestyle of service and personal growth as a productive partner in a mutually rewarding enterprise. The process of staff adjustment may be speeded up when the children under their care have few behavior and adjustment problems. In other words, it is easier for staff to adjust when the children are well behaved.

Developmental Cycle

In broad categories, the developmental cycle of children progresses from bonding (Birth to age 3), to personality development (Birth to age 5), to a knowledge base (Birth to age 7), to the basic aspects of character (Birth to 9), and the elements of spiritual formation (Birth to age 11). From age 12-14 peers begin to overly influence behavior as the child listens to and imitates those around them more than following the guidance of the caregiver. Then from age 15-18 they begin listening to other adults outside the original circle, the parents of friends or teachers at school. Sometimes, sadly, they listen to delinquents from the street instead of following the supervision of guardians and/or caregivers. However, by the time they face the real world around age 19, many if not most, have come to realize they cannot make it on their own and begin to fall back to the initial formative advice received from family, caregivers, and/or the formal guidance received during the process of development. At this point caring adults have another chance to influence their conduct and career.

The remedial development process depends on the age a child is removed from the birth-parent environment and the arrival age of entry into custodial care. First the physical health of the child must be determined. Then as part of the entry process to custodial care an honest assessment must be made as to the nature and level of **bonding** or lack thereof, that took place in the previous period, the degree and direction that **personality** had developed, the size of the educational and **knowledge base**, and the direction and level reached by **moral character and spiritual development**. It becomes obvious that the younger the age custodial care begins, the greater the possibility of repairing some of the broken or missing links and shoring up the basic building blocks neglected in a negative or neglected environment. It should be noted that when no positive steps were taken to develop these structures, the negative aspects of the environment did place some elements into the child's development.

As caregivers better understand the process and the logical movement from bonding, to personality, to knowledge base, to character and spiritual foundation, the better they can attempt to replace or repair the negative elements. Some of these steps are age-specific and if that age level has passed, the caregiver is limited in the amount of repair work that can be accomplished. Unless the substandard elements of the child's development are understood and corrected, a better quality of life may not be constructed. After one year of effort supported by affection and prayer if the assessment still shows major deficiencies, the child will need professional clinical attention which is normally beyond the ability of a custodial facility to provide.

One note of hope: when human efforts fail, there is divine intervention with authority and compassion to bring renewal, redemption, and restoration to the life of a child. Negative conditioning was not the fault or choosing of the children; therefore, an informed and affectionate caregiver plus a loving and powerful God can make a real difference. Do not neglect to ask for divine assistance in this difficult process.

Developmental Stages

These stages begin with the womb because a child learns a great deal prior to birth. Sounds, the mother's emotions, even the mother's diet and habits influence the development of a child. In fact, the logical development of a child begins in the lives of both parents prior to conception. At conception the gene pools of both parents are joined into one entity and the child will have DNA and traits traceable to parents and grandparents. When a child is born, a special human being enters the world, one that is different from all others that have ever or will ever walk this planet. Just as footprints; each child is different! Children are constructed from a gene pool that influences their basic traits and are placed in an environment that imprints their behavior. Children will develop in stages in a negative or positive direction depending on the weight of each factor.

- Womb to age 3 – essential human bonding
- Womb to age 5 – basic elements of personality
- Womb to age 7– layers for a knowledge base
- Womb to age 9 – rudimentary steps in character
- Womb to age 11 – keys to spiritual formation
- Age 12–14 – Peers influence more than adults
- Age 15–18 – Other adults influence conduct/career
- Age 19+ – Need a family anchor

SECTION ONE

(Womb to Age Three)
Essential Human Bonding

The Process of Remedial Bonding

Remedial bonding is a special intimacy that develops between a surrogate caregiver and a child. This bonding is tremendously important to the child's development. For most children this infant and/or 0-3 bonding relationship is their first and will affect all their future relationship issues. If the bond between the caregiver and child is one of love and security, then the child is more likely to seek out these healthy elements in future relationships. Children who miss quality infant bonding may grow up without the capacity for love and intimacy; therefore, bonding is the first and foremost responsibility of a custodial caregiver when a new child is placed in their care.

The Process of Bonding

Birth parents should begin working on the bonding connection months before the child is born. When this is missing and a child is placed in custodial care, "the sooner the better" is the rule for the remedial bonding process to begin. In fact, it is important to learn all the facts about the child before arrival at custodial care. Be certain plans for housing and care giving are arranged. Adequately prepare the staff and other children for the new arrival. Have a comfortable and secure place for the first night and day. Then show the child where they will "live" and introduce them to their "larger family." Condition the other children to be sensitive to the "new comer" and to welcome them into the family. However, permit the child to choose the ones with whom they wish to become close.

When a child arrives in custodial care during infancy the bonding process is more easily accomplished. However, all children are capable of and receptive to developing new relationships when their primary lodging is changed. This means that custodial and surrogate caregivers are able to form strong bonds even though they were not a part of prenatal and early infant bonding. Although it may be easier to establish a connection with younger children, there is no age cut-off. Interacting with and enjoying a child's company is critical to forming a bond. Infants should be cuddled or embraced. Children of walking age may resist a touch, but they like noises to get their attention and will play games in which you try to get the child to focus on you. If the child delights you and overwhelms you with feelings of love, this is a healthy sign indicating that you and your child are bonding. Should the child respond negatively to your touch, you must move carefully; most likely the child has been physically or sexually abused. Work through the process by permitting the child to make the first moves toward physical contact. This will help in the transition.

Birth Parent Neglect and Bonding

A dysfunctional childhood may result when bonding is neglected by birth parents. A disability may mean special challenges for surrogate parenting, but these can be overcome. If for example, your child has a communication or motor delay, he or she may have trouble expressing love for you. Instead of expecting full smiles and warm noises, you can learn to recognize smaller signals. A fleeting glance or even the movement of a finger can be as representative of love as are bigger gestures from older children. Be observant of all behavior; it is informative.

Research has validated that without a secure mother figure, a child who is exposed to unexpected events will have an intense stress reaction. When the umbilical cord is cut at birth, the physical attachment to the mother ceases, and the process begins for psychological and emotional attachment. The physical attachment in the womb was a life-sustaining connection necessary for birth, but the mental and emotional attachments that develop after birth are the forces that produce the quality of life. Without a firm bond to maternal affection, a child's personality, knowledge base, character, and spiritual formation and relationships will be difficult to influence positively.

Infants may become attached to a custodial caregiver. This attachment to a mother-figure brings a secure and safe base from which they can explore their surroundings. If they are adequately bonded, the child will seek the presence of the mother-figure when they are hurt, stressed or frightened. When the bonding is weak, the child may still seek the caregiver but may not receive the needed comfort or assurance. The absence of concrete bonding makes children less secure, their self-esteem is weakened, they are less self-reliant and often do not enjoy relationships with peers. Academic achievement is negatively impacted without concrete bonding, and for some reason it impacts a negative interest in math. It is obvious that bonding brings a sense of confidence to children and they are more apt to develop a positive attitude toward their surroundings.

Caregivers must realize that a lack of previous mother-figure bonding may have a long lasting effect on the child. They may become more anxious and insecure. However, a loving relationship that removes stress and provides secure surroundings will generate a sense of security and a less emotional response to the environment.

Reading and Bonding

Reading to and with a child is an uncomplicated way to establish a strong and nurturing caregiver/child connection. Reading and sharing stories with a child produces and enhances a positive bonding process. Several good children's books may be found at the Online Bookstore at **www.gea-books.com.**

Play and Bonding

With children play is natural, pleasant, and comforting. It may be difficult for an adult to get down on the floor, but eye-level playtime is important to children. During play children learn much about themselves, their environment and the people around them. Even the fantasy play of a young child is an effort to try on adult roles and skills for size. Play teaches self-control, the ability to take turns, and assists in seeing others viewpoint. Play enables a child to be more concerned about other, less aggressive physically, and more cooperative. When play is a two-way street, even more is learned and practiced that becomes helpful to the growing process. Play even increases their problem-solving skills for later.

Nature of Bonding

Bonding with a special needs child is most important. It is vital that caregivers understand the nature of bonding and how it impacts the emotional well-being of children. Bonding includes the formation of mutual emotional connections, and the giving of unconditional love flows in both directions. Bonding establishes emotional intimacy and a sense of closeness with a caregiver and produces a sense of security for the child. This intimacy builds the self-worth and self-image of the child and develops understanding and the ability for nonverbal communication to occur that gives a sense of belonging to a larger familial network. It works best when the connection is firmly established in the lives of all concerned.

Over-bonding

The presence of needy children can encourage extreme or over-bonding by a caregiver that creates an over-dependent relationship between caregiver and child. Because of special needs of a child, a caregiver may become too attentive and put the concerns of one child over the needs of others. This may happen when a caregiver feels grief-stricken over the past plight of the child and is tempted to overindulge or smother the child. This excess may develop a relationship that causes the child to be unable to build an individual personality or autonomy. In some cases such excess may neither encourage nor allow the child to accept personal responsibility for personal behavior. Over-bonding then becomes a negative influence on the child.

How to Recognize Bonding

All caregivers should review the signs for mutual bonding to assess the level of connection with the child. The level of bonding is manifested by the caregiver's attitude and interest in the child and the way the child is touched or held. The level of discomfort when the child leaves the caregiver for different surroundings speaks to this issue. The child's self-confidence, self-esteem, and sense of security in a social environment are signs of bonding.

A caregiver's over protective attitude can mean over-bonding. Acceptance, relaxation, and the ability to cope can mean normal bonding. Disinterest, indifference, negative response, and abandonment can mean a lack of bonding. When a mother-type or caregiver is permissive and pampering it can mean over-bonding. A normally bonded child is helpful, cooperative, and understanding. Blaming the child or condemning a child can slow the bonding process.

Roadblocks to Bonding

It takes something drastic to block the bonding of child and birth-mother. An unhealthy pregnancy can contribute to the problem, especially when parental anxiety results in blaming the child for the difficulties. Extreme discomfort in delivery can be a barrier to bonding. A premature birth or immediate medical needs interfere when the child is placed in post-natal intensive care unit that prevents touching, holding or rocking preventing healthy initial bonding. Early behavior problems can hinder bonding. When birth mothers use a child as a pawn in marital warfare, the bonding process is interrupted. If a child were to develop an unnatural feeling toward a birth-mother because of a feeling of rejection or abandonment, bonding is less than normal. A recognition of the obstructions to bonding can be used as a step toward improving the bonding process.

Steps toward Improved Bonding

Bonding can be improved with an infant or small child by following some simple rules. Place an infant on your chest area when both you and the child are relaxed so the child can hear and feel your heart beating. Physically touch and caress an infant and use hand massage techniques. Surround the small child with pleasant sounds and physically communicate face to face. Get down to the child's eye level and make face to face sounds. Try not to expect too much, but encourage the child to do all he or she is ready and capable of doing. Always speak in a loving and caring tone and show respect for the child's worth and value. Childlike behavior is normal. Do not force "adult-type" responses. Do child's play at the age-specific understanding and ability. Always listen to the mumbled language of a child; they are bright and have a language of their own. Talk gently with a child. You should always respond in a conversational tone. Permit children to grow and develop at their own pace. Teach children to sleep. A step by step program to teach a child to sleep well is needed.

SLEEPY TOWN

-- Lullaby and Story $19.95

This children's book uses the *Sleepy Town* lullaby as a guide and builds on the value of school, learning, and sharing what is learned with the family to establish a positive nighttime routine. The influence of the story will be experienced as the child learns to sing the song and the Sleepy Town Village story is read. Online Bookstore at www.gea-books.com

Sleepy Town
A Lullaby Song and Story
ZZ ZZZZZZZ ZZZZZ

HOLLIS L. GREEN

SECTION TWO

(Womb to Age Five)
Basic Elements of Personality

Remedial Development and Personality Development

Personality has elements of character, behavior qualities, and expressions of individuality and is recognizable soon after birth. It is the totality of one's attitudes, interests, physical behavioral patterns, emotional responses, social roles, and other individual traits that endure over time. Of the building blocks of personality, much is in place by age 5, but some later events impact the positive development of the adult personality.

If a child enters custodial care under five years of age, the caregiver needs to know how to assist with the building blocks of personality. If the child has passed the fifth birthday, then an assessment as to the degree personality development is appropriate in order to determine the remedial work that may be pursued. An assessment by a custodial caregiver relative to personality development will demonstrate where they must begin with remedial work in this difficult area. Clinically, it is a long and professional task to rebuild the personality of a neglected or abused child. Research has demonstrated that the lingering effect of physical and/or sexual abuse from family members remains even after a lifetime of positive and family relationships. Residual results may remain, but they no longer control the life and personality. Therefore, it is affirmed that affection and patience, time and energy, and secure and pleasant surroundings can move the task forward by replacing some of the bad stuff with better elements and enabling the person to cope with the realities of their present existence rather that dwelling on the negativity of the past. Additional effort in the arena of prayer and providence may do the rest – at least, all caregivers must do their best and leave the rest to a Higher Authority.

Knowing that a child does not think the same way as older siblings or an adult, has a shorter attention span, and sees the world through immature eyes can assist a caregiver in preparing listening and discussion sessions that can benefit the child. All children go through stages of growth and development on their way to becoming adults. Children are not miniature adults, they are immature and growing human beings grabbing on to every scrap of knowledge and bit of experience that can benefit their life. Caregivers must be conscious of the degree to which a child's personality has developed and that every human being is capable of growth and improvement in most areas of life.

Many adults unknowingly lead children astray through careless and inconsistent behavior. Such behavior can influence the future action of children for several generations. It seems that patterns of immoral attitudes, disrespectful behavior, and bad habits are passed to children and grandchildren from parents and grandparents (Exodus 20:5). Childhood is a crucial time for laying the proper foundation. Efforts to explain child development include listing the common characteristics of behavior by age groupings. It should be remembered however that every child will not fit into described patterns. Children grow and develop at different speeds and have a different set of influential factors coming from close family members. This material describes only general behavior and cohort groups often overlap.

Personality is Complex

There are multiple factors that shape a personality and usually come from heredity and environment. Personality is the complex of mental characteristics that makes individuals different from others. It includes all of the patterns of thought and emotions that cause one to say and do things in a particular style. At a basic level, personality is expressed through temperament, emotions and readily in-fluences values, beliefs, and expectations. Research over several decades has pointed to hereditary factors, espe-cially the basic emotional tone in the personality. Yet, it is equally evident that the acquisition of values, beliefs, hope, and outlook are greatly influenced by childhood socializa-tion and personal experiences. The gradual acceptance of the standard and practices of another culture influences personality development. Because of the pro-cess called enculturation, most individuals accept and adopt the tradi-tions, rules, manners, and biases of the culture in which they develop and grow. This fact gives custodial caregiv-ers a role in personal development of children.

Remedial personality development occurs through the interaction of temperament and environment. Temperament is the set of genetically determined traits that determine a child's approach to things and how the child learns about environment. There are no genes that specify personality traits, but some do control the development of the nervous system that controls behavior. Personality development in-cludes the caregiver working with the child to expand and enlarge certain processes such as the need for a growing readiness to express a sense of humor and to demonstrate a willingness to adapt to new situations. One needs a flexibility to preserve a predisposition to act positively and maintain connection with friends. It is necessary to widen the joy of reading to maintain mental stimulation. It is al-ways good to learn to live one day at a time and share with others. Maintain physical fitness through regular exercise and develop an awareness of what is happening. Always do things in moderation and cultivate hope in the future.

Many scholars agree that (1) temperament and (2) environment are influential in the development of human personality. **Temperament** depends on genetic factors and is often called <u>nature</u>, while the **environment** is called nurture. It is clear that both nature and nurture are factors in the development of personality in a child.

Crisis in Personal Development

Erik Erikson provided an early description of personality development in children. According to Erikson in 1956, the socialization process of an individual consists of eight steps, each one accompanied by an emotional and a social crisis that must be resolved for the child to adequately handle the next stage of development. These phases drastically impact personality development, with five occurring during infancy, childhood, and adolescence-- a time period most relevant to the custodial caregiver.

Stage One: Infancy – When an infant is well-nurtured and loved during the first two years of life, they develop **hope** by learning basic trust. When these first two years are influenced by bad parenting and a negative environment, the infant becomes insecure and learns to mistrust which is the opposite of hope. To have hope one must develop two things: desire and expectancy. When children desire and expect a good response from a caregiver they develop hope, when they are disappointed they develop mistrust.

Stage Two: Toddlerhood – The second stage begins when the child is almost two years old and lasts until age four. The early part of this stage may include tantrums, stubbornness, and negativism depending on the child's temperament. This early phase may influence negative parenting responses and thus influence the child's future. This stage is when a toddler develops **autonomy** (self-sufficiency and independence) or a **sense of shame** (discomfort, humiliation, or embarrassment). This is when the "human will" is developed that produces will-power, resolve, or spirit which provides a child's enthusiasm. A well-parented child emerges from this phase with self-confidence, happy with his/her newly found control.

However, negative parenting behavior during the early stage of this phase can greatly harm personality develop-ment.

Stage Three: Preschool – The early part of the third stage is considered the "play phase" or the later preschool years from about age three to the formal entry into school. This is when a child develops a **sense of purpose** and goes through a learning initiative or guilt period where a child learns the words fault, blame, and experiences the feeling of remorse or sorrow. The child learns broader skills through play and fantasy, to use imagination, to cooperate with others, and to lead as well as follow. If this phase is not adequately negotiated, the child may depend excessively on adults, become fearful, refuse to join groups, harbor feelings of guilt, and may learn the experiential meaning of the words, such as, fault and blame as they feel remorse or sorrow.

Stage Four: Primary School Age – This stage has to do with competence and relates to learning or inferiority developed during primary school age. The child learns to master more formal skills such as moving from free play to structured play or team sports, and learning basic academic skills (reading, writing, and arithmetic). Any faith-based spiritual formation will not come from the school system; it must be supplied by the family or caregiver. During this phase the need for self-discipline grows each year. The child who has adequately negotiated the earlier stages will be trusting, autonomous, industrious, and filled with initiative. Where failure has occurred in an earlier step, the child will feel inferior, will mistrust others, and have doubts about the future.

Stage Five: Adolescence – This fifth stage relates to learning identity and is pushed in different directions. From about age 12 to 14 the process of maturity begins and the adolescent is pulled and pushed among many emotions and commitments: loyalty, reliability, trustworthiness, devotion, and conformity. The adolescent acquires a self-certainty as opposed to doubts and experiments with various constructive roles rather than accepting a negative identity. The well-adjusted adolescent avoids delinquency and looks toward achievement. Later in the period a clear sexual identity is established. Caregivers begin to inspire, and gradually ideals to live by are formulated. Assisting a child through the various stages of emotional and personality development is a complex and difficult task.

Although scholars do not always agree on the process of development, they normally agree that there are critical periods in personality development and that a child will be more sensitive to guidance factors during these times. Most agree that a child's needs should be met in a family-type environment or at least in a wholesome custodial environment that attempts to maintain a family-type atmosphere. Culture becomes an important environmental factor. Europe and the United States of America have maintained individualistic cultures and emphasized individual needs. In contrast, Asia, Africa, Central and South America are characterized by community-centric cultures that focus on belonging to a larger group, such as family or nation. In such cultures, cooperation is more important than competitiveness, and this necessarily affects personality development.

Traits Related to Personality

Infants display differences between each other in activity levels, responsiveness to change, and irritability level. Some cry constantly while others seem happy. Research has identified five traits in a young child that may facilitate or hinder personality development. They are:

1. How sensitive the child is to touch, taste, smell, sound, and light..

2. The general level of activity and how vocal they become.

3. The ability to pay attention when the child is not interested or level of stubbornness.

4. The predictability of appetite and sleep.

5. How easily a child adapts to changes or strangers and overall tendency to be positive or negative.

General Concerns about Personality Development

Most children experience healthy personality development, but those with developmental disorders have difficulty dealing with others. They tend to be inflexible, rigid, and unable to respond to the changes and normal stresses of life and find it difficult to participate in social activities. When these characteristics are present in a child to an extreme, when they are persistent, and when they interfere with healthy development, a diagnostic evaluation with a clinical professional is recommended. It is an important first step in knowing whether there is a disorder and, if so, what treatment is best for the child. Child and adolescent professionals are trained to sort out whether or not a child's personality development is normal.

SECTION THREE

(Womb to Age Seven)
Layers for a Knowledge Base

Building a Knowledge Base

The knowledge base consists of the short-term memory of facts, information, and data that are used to create the long-term memory that produces competency based knowledge that is relatively permanent. Creative or divergent thinking is not done in a vacuum. It depends on and uses a knowledge base. There is too much emphasis on trying to understand the process purely from a procedural perspective and not from the point of view of the necessary knowledge base. Close observation of the creative thinking processes of children illustrates clearly the critical role of the knowledge base.

Children, over time, develop a core competency baseline that feeds a knowledge base upon which they will construct most of the future information that formal education and reading supplies. At age 7 or about the time a child enters the third year of school, the foundation baseline should be established, and they should be able to read and write at an appropriate level in order to proceed higher in the educational structure. Early instruction and the development of reading and comprehension skills build the base for the competency baseline. The more and better a child reads, the firmer the knowledge base becomes.

Engagement in reading is the key to developing the competency baseline. The ability to construct the meaning from the text is a learning process that is active, cognitive, and affective. Background knowledge and prior experience are critical to reading and developing the baseline for competency. Reading and writing are complementary processes where the development of one improves the other. Reading and writing involve complex thinking and enhance social interaction that is essential to all stages of intellectual development.

When an environment is rich in the experience of reading and writing with available resources and opportunities to read, a child learns productive strategies both in and out of school. When parents and caregivers read to children and personally demonstrate an interest in reading, children learn to associate letters with the speech sounds they represent. The phonemic awareness is a step toward learning to recognize the whole word as a unit and thus develop construct recognition which is essential to learning and utilizing the knowledge base. Children need a variety of strategies to model and demonstrate reading knowledge and skills. Children need opportunities to read and this reading process and competency should be monitored and evaluated to be certain the knowledge base is firm and growing.

Why do we say that children should read at a certain level by the end of the third school year? The linguistic and cognitive demands on children after the third year of school are drastically changed. During the first three years of school, children are learning to read after this point a transition is made and children read to learn. This is why the knowledge base at age 7 is critical to the educational and functional future of a child. Time moves forward in one direction. Children who read and write below a core competency baseline are left behind as the "readers" move on. Without this competency base, children cannot negotiate the transition from reading narrative or storybook prose to the level of an expository or informational text.

A surrogate caregiver needs to discover a new child's reading experience. Usually, a neglected child is also deficient in reading skills. In a negative environment the reading experience has most likely been limited, frustrating, and unfulfilling. This means the child's vocabulary is probably not up to grade level and the child has not developed an ability to enjoy literature.

When a child is deficient in reading and writing skills, it normally means limited exposure to new words, books, and text. Any prediction about the child's future academic performance is negative and seriously jeopardized by difficulties in reading and writing. Can the caregiver bring the child up to speed in these knowledge areas so the child can become an adequate reader by the end of the third year of school? Has the child passed the third year of school? Can you, as caregiver, do the remedial work necessary to construct a stronger knowledge base and create an interest and a willingness to read and write and grow in vocabulary and comprehension ability? A child's language and expression skills and enjoyment of literature are supported and reinforced by the ability to read fluently. A goal of the caregiver is to provide the child the skills needed to become a good reader.

Instruction in reading is an essential part of remedial childcare. Reading is the doorway to learning. It is though reading that children gain access to history, politics, literature, news, and information. Without the ability to read well, it is difficult to become an adequate achiever. Reading is power. It is critical for self-improvement, self-awareness, and self-determination and is related to self-trust. Not only does reading provide access to the world, it opens the door to the inner self and provides a confidence that permits trust in others. When children are limited in the area of reading, they have limited choices in life. Research supports the urgency of early instruction in reading. Children in the bottom one-fourth of the reading continuum are more likely to fail or become an early dropout of school. Dropping out of school often means abandoning hope for the future or literally dropping out of life.

The knowledge base upon which children build their life is formed from birth to about age 7. After this time, most of what is learned is related to something they already know. The earlier a child reads well, the higher the projection of achievement in school and life. Reading well is not only knowing the words but recognizing them in time to read with speed. Bad reading habits and poor reading skills relate to both comprehension and speed and tend to persist even as a child moves up to the next level in the system. This becomes an academic handicap that is most difficult to overcome. And because of what some call, social promotion, no noteworthy effort is made to solve the poor reader's problems even when it is clearly known that the child will have continued difficulty with reading and life.

Children without adequate word recognition skills read less, read slowly, have slower development of vocabulary, and are less motivated to read. A fluency of about 40 correct words recognized per minute by the end of grade one is the benchmark. Limitations in early reading ability can result in great differences in the amount of reading during the early years. This limited reading impacts the knowledge base and thus produces limitations for the child's future development. In addition it is clear that the information available in the knowledge base exerts a significant influence on the acquisition and retention of future information.

SECTION FOUR

(Womb to Age Nine)
Rudimentary Steps in Character Building

Remedial Development and Character

Character is the set of affective, cognitive, and behavioral patterns gleaned from life experience that determines how one thinks, feels, and behaves. Character continues to develop throughout life, although much depends on inborn traits and early childhood experiences. Character is also related to the level of moral development. While the debate continues as to which of these provide the most influence, most scholars agree that proper parenting and good childcare are critical to the development of a child's character. Caregivers who have the facts and can adapt surrogate parenting to the temperament and environment of the child can provide better environment and guidance and influence the development of good character and a mature attitude toward the world.

SECTION FIVE

(Womb to Age Eleven)
Keys to Spiritual Formation

Development and Spiritual Formation

Just as all the other steps in development, spiritual formation begins before birth and continues through about age eleven. Spiritual formation is influenced by significant events in the life of the child, personal experiences, parental and adult behavior, observation of peers, and social changes in or near their early environment. Parents and caregivers have become specialists in nutrition. Learning disorders and new guidance techniques have been established. Children are enrolled, coached, and transported to and from school, music lessons, games, practices, social events, medical appointments, but in many respects parents and caregivers are missing the core of the child's needs: personal spirituality.

Spirituality in Children

Normally children were thought to be too self-centered to process supernatural abstracts or theoretical concepts. Scholars believed children just absorbed values and beliefs from their parents or caregivers. More recently research has demonstrated that pre-school children are interested in both the supernatural and the nature of being, and this includes right and wrong, good and evil, life and death, and the existence of God. Children want to make the world have meaning.

It is important to note that all spiritual formation is not positive; it depends on the person or persons providing the information and the context in which the concept and constructs related to spirituality are presented. Spiritual formation is a central aspect of development and takes place both negatively and positively in all children regardless of age, faith-based connections, basic beliefs, family values, or worldview. Spirituality is not age-specific; it relates more to maturity and knowledge than to age. Most children have an inner clock and an inner compass that guides their life, but sometimes they must be instructed to observe those inner impulses.

When a child asks, "Would it be wrong for me to do....?" It is a good sign that the inner soul light is burning. A wise proverb (Proverbs 20:27) states, "The spirit of man is the candle of the Lord searching all the inner parts..." Everyone, including children, has a conscience that searches out the inner bad stuff. This inner spirit leads in the direction of the good path unless older people teach children bad habits and permit them to make poor choices. At times the word spiritual is too comprehensive a concept for the young to grasp, so one speaks of being good, obeying your parents, listening to your teacher, not taking things that do not belong to you, or telling things that are not true. These steps build character and the elements of character are the basic building blocks of spiritual formation.

Perhaps one would not find their way through this world without some aspects of spiritual formation. The secular folk may want to call it only character, but that is the place good things start. A person of good character is just a small step from being spiritual. The ingredients of spiritual formation slip into a child's life at the early stages of development often without the child's knowledge. Normally the adults do not see any verbal indications that the idea or concept has taken hold, but the seeds are planted.

The Greek version of "spiritual" was illustrated by what they called awareness. The Greeks had three aspects of this awareness: 1) awareness of self, 2) awareness of self in the world, and 3) awareness of a god or higher power.

When a person realized the value of self, and understood that the higher power had placed him/her in the world for a purpose, and that the world was made by this higher power, the emotion was felt in what the Greeks called the heart. These steps may be similar to spiritual awareness. Spirituality is personal awareness of who one is and just that knowledge is what it means to be alive and spiritually aware of higher things. Consider the steps more closely.

First, self-awareness or self-worth and self-esteem are the essential ingredients of spirituality. Second, an awareness of the awesome world in which one exists and moves in time and space. Finally, awareness that a higher power has placed us in this world for a purpose: the emotion felt in the heart when all this awareness comes together is the fountainhead of spirituality. Most everyone has his or her own way of feeling spiritual and caregivers must never impose their version of private or faith-based religiosity on a child. Personal spirituality is much like "hash in grandma's kitchen," it accumulates over time and grandma mixes a little love and seasoning with the hash to make it good to the taste and nutritious and serves it hot with love. This is the nearest explanation available to explain spirituality in children. A caregiver should only answer the questions that the Spirit prompts the child to ask. Spiritual things must accumulate within each child and should be kindled by the Holy Spirit and warmed by the affection of a mature caregiver.

Some children tend to identify spirituality with having made an intentional choice to accept an offer of salvation, etc. Developing a spiritual nature is much more than an event, a decision; it is an ongoing life-style and becomes a part of the fabric of one's being and the essence of who one really is. Being spiritual is not following or obeying rules; it is having a change of heart that causes one to want to obey and follow the right path through all aspects of life. This provides one with purpose and direction for life.

With emerging research to convince custodial care personnel that giving attention to spirituality in children really matters, it still takes courage for custodial care in a pluralistic society to adopt spirituality as a natural dimension of development. This is distinct from sectarian religion or practicing the faith of a particular denomination; it has to do with full personal development in the area of morality, ethics, and faith-based living. The goal of remedial and surrogate parenting in custodial care is to establish sound ethical foundations for the children.

Nurturing children spirituality is done by listening to every word they speak, exposing them to nature, helping them expand their imagination, encouraging their dreams and celebrating the good things that happen in their life. These are gifts that will last a lifetime and could be the most precious legacy a parent or caregiver passes to a child.

Caregivers and Spiritual Formation

Caregivers should never talk directly about spirituality, instead they should watch for an opportunity to cultivate natural interest in honesty, fairness, morality, ethics, and justice. Custodial personnel should articulate their own spiritual autobiography or journey and share it with other staff members. The vocabulary used and any diversity between behavior and experiences would become obvious. Identify common difficulties such as death of a love one, loss of job, or other experiences that impact the way one thinks about God and justice. Do not seek consensus, but wrestle with the relationship between religion and spirituality and understanding the difference. Provide literature and other reading material. Review the child development process and see if workers can think of ways and means to introduce the constructs and building blocks of spirituality into the custodial care program. The big question: can your facility establish a climate and practice that respects and nurtures spiritual development across the cultural and faith-based environment? What are the ethical boundaries? What resistance do they anticipate?

Childcare is well-fitted to contribute to the spiritual development of children in a pluralistic environment. Normally, children are received from various backgrounds, and this makes it important that pluralism is noted. All custodial care workers should be aware that the capacity to recognize and nurture the spiritual development of others grows with critical attentiveness to one's own spiritual journey.

Once the confidence is gained to introduce spiritual development to the personnel in a custodial care facility, it is ongoing and automatic. It equips workers to be careful about their own spiritual life and professional services while it creates an environment conductive to the construction of a healthy community in which children may thrive and grow. Some theorists consider spirituality to be biologically natural or inbuilt in humans, closely linked to a child's simplicity and sense of wonder. Research has discovered high levels of spirituality in children under thirteen and a sharp decline of spirituality in adolescence.

SECTION SIX

(Age 12 to 14)
Peer Group Influence

Monitor Adverse Peer Influence on Children

Among the most destructive things that can happen to a child is to become socially involved with peers who have bad habits, immoral behavior and weak character. In the general population it is difficult to restrict these associations because the restriction has the reverse effect. This means that the associates of children and adolescents must be monitored and each negative incident promptly dealt with by a loving parent. This is where the custodial environment has an advantage. The caregivers in the custodial arena can control the associations within the facility, but when children go to public school the same problems exist as parents have with their children's association with bad company. It becomes necessary to use tough love and explain to a child or adolescent that some associations are unacceptable. Things they want to do and some people with whom they want to associate are not good. Constructive communication is crucial at this point.

Early adolescence peer groups have a considerable influence on other children's behavior. Some peer groups are involved in deviant and aggressive behavior while other peer groups have acceptable social behavior. The first group is made up of adolescents who were popular and the second group was made of the kind of nice kids that everyone likes. The first group, made up of deviant and aggressive young teens, was noted for theft and skipping school, being physically aggressive and starting fights, and socially aggressive by excluding others from their group. Over a period of months, individuals in a particular group tend to become more similar in behavior to others in the group and to a greater extent in the aggressive group. Children want to belong to a popular group and the peer pressure from the group to conform, accounts for the influence of such groups. Children in the group of nice kids are harmfully affected only when the group as a whole dislikes other groups. Members of deviant and disliked groups even though they maintained popularity, usually became more deviant over time. Caregivers must provide constructive guidance to peer associations.

SECTION SEVEN

(Age 15 to 18)
Other Adult Role Models

Other adult role models such as teachers, the parents

of peers, etc. begin to have significant influence. What custodial care plans to do to prepare children for the real world must be done prior to age 15 or a new and special program must be established to deal with changes in adolescent behavior.

SECTION EIGHT

(Age 19 +)
Stop the World, I Want to get off!

By age 19 young people have learned the cost of going to school, driving a car, or living in their own place. They often return to parents, grandparents or custodial personnel for assistance with school or living expenses. This should not be discouraged. It gives the family or custodial care a "second chance" to influence their future.

Once young people have come to the stage of wanting to stop the world and get off, they are usually open to mature family guidance about the future. The world can be a scary place for young people and unless they have a family anchor, they will turn to artificial support that leads to becoming involved with the wrong people.

See this second chance as an opportunity and an obligation. It is probably the last chance the family or custodial care personnel will have to influence and guide the young person before they take a permanent place in society. Everyone should assume that "place" will be a constructive and productive member of society. Any negativity passed to a young person at this stage most likely will be counterproductive. Be positive. Philosophy taught that one could never reach a positive conclusion beginning with a negative premise. The old proverb "accentuate the positive and eliminate the negative" is still a good guideline for caregivers.

Like footprints each child is different!

CHAPTER SIX

REMEDIAL AND SURROGATE PARENTING

General parenting skills relate directly to the tutorial process. Remember the definition of parenting: the experiences, skills, qualities, and responsibilities involved in being a legal guardian and in teaching and/or caring for a child. Parents are the primary teachers for children and most of the knowledge base that a child has is founded on the guidance of parents, caregivers, and early teachers. Parenting as well as tutoring requires both maternal and paternal natural instincts even if there is only one person available to tutor and nurture the child in custodial care.

A good example of a man having both mothering instincts and fatherly discipline is made clear in the life and letters of St. Paul. In First Thessalonians 2:7,8 (EDNT) Paul wrote of his maternal affection, "We were tender among you, even as a nursing **mother** warmly takes pleasure in her children; so affectionately longing for you, we were willing to share with you, not only the gospel of God, but also well pleased to share our lives, because you were valued by us." Then verses 11,12 (EDNT) Paul wrote of his paternal concern, "As you know how we encouraged, comforted, and charged every one of you, as a **father** treats his children, that you would lead a life worthy of God, who has called you unto the glory of his kingdom." Since such a great leader of the pristine church could be both mother and father to young converts, surely those providing custodial care for children can allow both maternal and paternal instincts to function in producing care, comfort, and discipline for the children for whom they are responsible. Children are much like sheep: they need both a shepherd to guide them toward green pastures and fences to establish boundaries as they walk through the valley and shadows of evil that will keep them on the "straight and narrow way."

Shepherd and Fences

Some years ago traveling by train from London to Birmingham, England, many sheep were along the rail lines. My knowledge of sheep was limited to the facts in the Bible. The only thing known was that sheep needed a shepherd. Seeing many sheep, but no shepherds, an English traveling companion was asked, "Are the shepherds on strike?" The answer was firm and clear: "We don't have shepherds; we have fences." With this knowledge, my understanding of sheep was expanded. Sheep must have either a shepherd or a fence or perhaps both. Children need both the care of a shepherd/caregiver and the restriction of fences/rules!

Just how does a caregiver create an atmosphere conducive to remedial and productive development? There are several steps in this process if it is to influence both cognitive and affective development.

1. First one must establish good rapport with the child and cultivate a genuine friendship.
2. Learn to control the behavior of a child without fear

through a "kind and gentle spirit" and in the spirit of the Good Shepherd who said, "Suffer little children to come unto me!"

3. Carefully establish rules and boundaries of behavior. This is best done by example. Children learn first by imitation. The bad you see in the child is most likely an imitation of what was witnessed in the previous environment. A poem by an unknown author speaks to this issue:

    With all the mess in the papers,
    One can't blame the kitten's capers,
    When making noise and trouble too,
    While copying what the old cats do!

4. Give the child something good and wholesome to imitate.

5. Generally establish a daily routine with standardized activities. Children appreciate discipline; it makes them feel safe. A standardized routine is the best way to establish a good habit. It often takes 21-days to establish a good habit, but only one incident to break that habit. Therefore, be easy in your judgment. A child will make mistakes. It is helpful if the caregiver finds a way to minimize the mistakes. Always take the "lemon and make lemonade!"

6. Understand the force of the affective domain in reaching the inner core of the child at the feeling level. A child operates on feelings. No matter how bright they are or how high their I.Q. may be, children are reached first through their feelings. Learn to read the unspoken emotional language of the child. This is the language of the heart.

7. Establish an emotional, social, and spiritual connection. Connect with the child at as many levels as possible. Be friendly! Be happy! Be honest! Be fair! Be a good witness of your faith-based

experience! Be a good example. Use the obvious failure of others as "Good bad examples" for the child to avoid.

Lead by example in every aspect of both personal and professional life. Children must never witness inconsistency in the caregiver. Children placed in custodial care have already seen sufficient discrepancy and contradiction in their previous environment. Your influence is positive when you are a good example in all aspects of life.

Affective Direction in Surrogate Care

A basic assumption in surrogate care is that a child's behavior and achievement are governed by a feeling of well-being. Understanding the affective domain provides useful information for those who guide children in personal growth and academic development.

There must be a formalized program stressing supportive behavior and a continuing dialogue between caregiver and child to enhance both learning and human relationships in the affective domain. This deals constructively with a sensitivity to art and beauty, interpersonal relations, moral/ethical development, and self-knowledge. It is strongly affirmed that the most purposeful goals to be carried out in the custodial care arena should include the concurrent development of intellectual skills with emotional behaviors by encouraging children to think and feel about their life and present values.

To improve the knowledge of the affective domain in child development, a planning and tutoring model with general application is needed. A scheme for classifying and organizing tutorial/learning material must be established that will chart the scope and sequence of instruction and guidance. A tutorial design based on child developmental theory could provide the tools and a sense of direction that makes it possible for caregivers of children to prepare and implement instructional and discussion sessions.

Tutorial goals are needed to assist learners in recognizing and understanding emotions, attitudes, and values and how their surroundings and associations with others influence what they say and do. The tutorial goals should make children aware of the outcomes and consequences that may result from feelings of joy, anger, fear, surprise, or distress. Caregivers need to tutor children to weigh the outcome of decisions with reference to the effect choices may have on them and others and recognize the different ways that they could respond. Finally, children must understand the nature, forms, and consequences of aggression and apply their knowledge of emotions, attitudes, and values toward positive, real-life experience. It is a "learn as you do" process.

An effective surrogate care model will assist children with their self-concept, interpersonal relationship with peers, and how they feel about the custodial environment. This aesthetic sensitivity determines, to a large extent, the degree of motivation the child has to achieve a learning objective. It deals with both thinking and feeling. Proceeding from what is known and accepted to the unknown is standard practice in education. A mixture of models may be used in planning a course of action which leads to tutoring in both the cognitive and affective domains. This means planning and tutoring for both thinking and feeling.

Automatic Response Tutorial System

Synergetic methodology is an automatic response tutorial system that combines the efforts of two or more persons. It is sophisticated but not complicated. When one understands how the structure works; it is simple. Knowing the needs of children in a learning environment and having a grasp of the child development process makes the automatic response system work. When one works with a system that produces a synergy or "working together," the learning and developmental aspects of custodial care are simplified. Synergy occurs when two or more forces work together and the combined efforts are greater than the sum of the individual efforts. The process of custodial care for remedial development works when the caregiver and child act in harmony with unity of purpose and the objectives, goals, and standard are clearly understood.

Learning from one another has great impact on children at times for good, at other times for bad. Children learn bad habits and vocabulary from other children; while children are susceptible to bad influence, they want to learn everything new. That is where the tutor and caregiver enter the picture. In a positive instructional and guidance environment, children can learn the essential content to reach age-specific levels of development.

Synergetic tutoring is an approach to custodial care in which children in small cohort groups learn from one another through structured interactions and tutorial guidance; thus, the idea of synergy in learning. Challenge and stimulation are created through social situations where real and felt needs can be both discussed and satisfied. Custodial care must provide learning activities and materials from which knowledge or insights can be acquired and present tutorial instructions for both the individual child and age cohort learning groups.

Planning Process Determines Action

In the arena of human development a parent or person serving as a caregiver, teacher, or custodial authority must first become a "friend to the child" then assume the role of a parent, schoolyard policemen, or even a teacher. First this person or persons must become a "friend" of the child by simply being friendly. Ancient sacred text declared, "He who has friends, must show himself friendly." The big question is how do friends treat friends?

God does not make junk. When a child is trashed or abandoned, some adult is responsible; it is not the child's fault. Although the child will most likely feel guilty and sincerely believe he/she has done something wrong. This is especially true if there has been physical or sexual abuse in the previous environment. The background, previous surroundings, and the present physical and mental condition of the child must take priority as the caretaker builds rapport and becomes friends with the child.

Structure of Thinking and Learning

Models provide visual representations of related concepts and simplify complex notions placing them within view. To illustrate the three components of mental functioning, J. P. Guilford devised a cube-shaped model. Each dimension of the cube represented a function of the mind, hence a three dimensional model.

A partial representation of the J. P. Guilford's model.

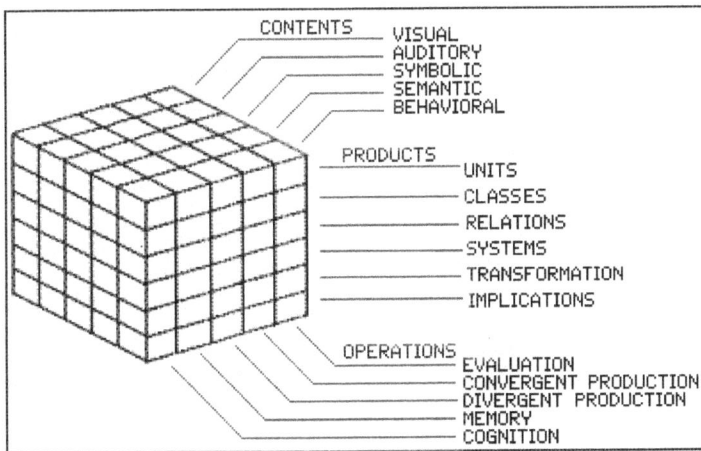

Figure 7

In Guilford's Model, intelligence is viewed as comprising operations, contents, and products. There are 5 kinds of **operations** or ways of thinking (cognition, memory, divergent production, convergent production, evaluation),

6 kinds of **products** or basic units of thought known as constructs (units, classes, relations, systems, transformations, and implications), and 5 kinds of **contents** or information and anything that is known (visual, auditory, symbolic, semantic, behavioral). Since each dimension is independent, there are theoretically 150 different components of intelligence. This is why building the knowledge base is vital to the future development of a child.

Implementation of Cognitive and Affective Behaviors

Using Guilford's three-dimensional model, Frank E. Williams prepared a plan for teaching and learning. The Williams "Cube" visually portrays a plan for cultivating creative-productive thinking in the traditional content areas. Three important aspects of Williams' model should be noted: (1) An emphasis is on the higher level thought processes, creative thinking. (2) A teacher is given a choice of instructional strategies. (3) The cognitive and affective processes are represented in combination.

In breaking away from strict cognitive emphasis, Williams took a pioneering step. Williams showed that it was possible to develop both the thinking and feeling processes in association with the learning of subject/content. This model clearly portrays the three dimensions of teaching and learning. These dimensions may be incorporated into a Model for Implementing Cognitive Affective Behaviors. It is important that they be understood: (1) **Content** - traditional subject matter, (2) **Tutor behavior** --ways of tutoring and guiding children, and (3) **Learner behavior** -- ways of thinking and feeling. Having established a three dimensional framework for model building, it now becomes necessary to touch base with established plans for cognitive and affective development. Originally written as a plan to classify levels of mental operations, Taxonomy has proven to be a valuable working tool for instructional planners and content builders. The taxonomical classification of learning goals provides for an upward progression from "the recall of information" to "making judgments." The progression is from the simple to the complex.

The Cognitive Taxonomy is of value to tutors in the following ways: (1) It establishes a learning order and moves from the lower to the higher order thinking processes. (2) It may be used to prepare objectives because it suggests learning outcomes. (3) It provides a target for clarifying desired learner behavior. (4) When appropriate "cueing verbs" are used to direct or prompt learner behavior, the outcome is predictable. Using "cueing verbs" is of great assistance to children in a remedial learning situation.

Affective Domain

Educational literature often refers to the whole learner, the total person, or the whole being. More recently, tutors were introduced to the notion of Holistic Learning. The intent is to acknowledge all qualities of the learner, not just the academic. Considering the affective domain, makes provision to take into consideration the values and influence of the child's feelings about the subject and the situation.

Much the same as the Cognitive Taxonomy, the Affective Taxonomy provides a useful way to describe and classify learning objectives. For remedial tutors it has practical value. When used as a resource guide, it becomes possible to design instruction, which focuses on the non-intellectual aspects of individual growth and development. Such practices as the improvement of self-concept, enhancing interpersonal relationships, and dealing with moral issues no longer need to be left to accident or chance.

The Affective Taxonomy is useful to caregivers and tutors in the following ways:

1. A resource guide for session planning.
2. A system for organizing learning materials.

3. A plan for establishing tutorial materials. (4) A way of comparing teaching and learning styles. And (5) A target for composing and directing cueing words to prompt a child to recall a process or rule.

Operational Definitions of Cognitive Goals

The cognitive goals that appear in the left hand column are in summary form. The operational definitions in the right hand column suggest behavior related to each goal. The goals and operational definitions are in ascending order 1 to 6.

Cognitive Goals:	Operational Definitions:
6. Evaluation – Judgment in terms of internal and external criteria.	>6. The child decides, a judgment of right and wrong, good or bad is based on established criteria.
5. Synthesis – Production of a unique communication, plan or set of operations	>5. The child creates a product or designs a unique plan.
4. Analysis -- Breakdown of communication into elements, relationships, organization.	>4. The child reasons and determines parts, order, and relationships.
3. Application – Use abstractions in particular and concrete situations.	>3. The child applies information and uses it to solve problems.
2. Comprehension – Lowest level of understanding; information is translated and interpreted	>2. The child explains and demonstrates his/her understanding.
1. Knowledge – Involves the recall of specifics, terms, facts, and methods.	>1. The child knows.

Operational Definitions for Affective Goals

The affective goals in the left column are in summary form.   The operational descriptions in the right column suggests the disposition, attitude, and feelings of the child associated with each goal. The goals and responses are ascending 1 to 5.

<u>Affective Goals:</u>

<u>Operational Definitions:</u>

5.Characterization>>>>
Internalization of a value.
Value system consistent with
behavior.

5. The child voices belief
and affirms values.

4. Organization >>>>>>
Recognize pervasive values,
determines Inter-relationships
of values, organizes value
systems.

4. The child reviews, questions,
and arranges values into an
ordered system or plan.

3. Valuing >>>>>>>>>>
Accepting, preferring, and
making commitment to a
value.

3. The child chooses a concept
or behavior believed to be
worthy.

2. Responding >>>>>>
Willingness to respond,
motivated, gains satisfaction if
responding

2. The child wants to discuss or
explain.

1.   Receiving >>>>>>>>
Pays attention, is aware,
takes information into
account.

1. The child displays
attentiveness; listens, notices,
and observes.

I will not yell at a child;

I will not throw things;

I will not tease the children.

I am a surrogate parent-teacher,

— I am the caregiver!

This I promise.

Like footprints each child is different!

CHAPTER SEVEN

LONG-TERM ASPECTS OF CHILD DEVELOPMENT

Anger and Frustration

Anger and frustration are normal responses to the neglect and abuse of children prior to their arrival in custodial care. Although such behavior is illegal it is seldom punished. You may ask Why not? There is no system to instruct new parents how to raise an infant and no effort to correct the faulty behavior and the poor parenting by the birth parents. Consequently, many children are marked for life by the negative input of a dysfunctional environment and flawed guardianship. These parents are not mean or bad people; just ignorant of the parenting process or simply perpetuating the negative environment in which they themselves were raised. It is this cycle that surrogate parenting must break if a child is to have a positive future and become a productive member of society.

Two Broad Terms

Determinism and Purposive Control are broad terms used to explain the long-term aspects of human development. Child caregivers need to understand both concepts and how these concepts may assist the construction of a remedial development process for neglected or abused children. An understanding of both constructs may impact remedial and surrogate parenting in a custodial environment. One does not have to be a specialist in psychology (study of the mind), sociology (the study of groups), or social psychology (study of individuals in the context of groups) to become an exceptional caregiver for children. All that is really needed is basic human instincts that are inborn patterns of behavior necessary to survival and reproduction. As long as the caregiver permits these natural gifts and skills to work that are normally exercised in both the maternal and paternal aspects of parenting, they may function well in the custodial arena. In addition to the inborn and natural instincts, caregivers need an awareness of current research and knowledge relative to remedial and surrogate parenting.

Determinism is a broad term with a variety of meanings for parenting skills. Corresponding to these different meanings is a different understanding of the facts. **Causal determinism** argues that future events are always determined by the past. This is a kind of rear view mirror effect that determines individual response to a given stimuli or situation. When certain things happen, it may trigger an old response to even new situations. Caregivers must be aware that this "rear view mirror effect" often determines the child's behavior at a given moment in time, but new and positive experiences can alter the results. **Logical determinism** is the notion that all intentions (propositions), whether about the past, present or future, are either positive or negative. As the caregiver learns the facts about a child's past environment, these facts will naturally be classified as either good or bad for the child. This information may then be used in discussion sessions with the child and good can be used to reinforce the positive and the bad used as a good "bad example" of negative behavior. **Theological determinism** postulates that God determines all that humans will do, either by knowing their actions in advance, via some form of omniscience or by decreeing their actions in advance. It is true that God has a purpose for each life. Theological determinism does not negate free will. God gives each one a free will that produces the power of choice. Just remember that God does not make junk. Garbage accumulates in a bad environment. Providence desire only the best for all human beings; and that includes the children of the world. God never intended for a child to be raised in substandard conditions by less than adequate parenting or by a neutral state that simply warehouses children until they are old enough to work. Perhaps more appropriate to the remedial and surrogate caregiver is a positive answer to these questions:

1. Do individuals have control over the acts that determine their future?

2. Does a caregiver have the potential to undo or override the negative programming of a child and thus affect a better and more productive future?

Understanding Purposive Control

Purposive Control advocates claim that individuals make choices that affect their personal future. These options have negative or positive outcomes. In a dysfunctional family environment, children have no choices. In the arena of custodial care, one of the greatest problems is facilitating the desire to make good choices by the child. The ability to choose one thing, a person, or a course of action in preference to others is a mark of maturity. The ability and/or opportunity to choose generates growing power. Learning to choose the best or most desirable path forward is good assurance that the future will be better than the past.

One cannot be effective in purposive control unless they understand the purpose. It is the reason for which something exists or for which it has been made. In life, purpose becomes the long-range direction one may travel to reach desired objectives and goals. Therefore, assisting children in determining objectives and establishing goals for the future become good milestones on the journey of life. Not only do individuals need to understand their purpose in life and develop objectives and establish goals, they must understand that there are standards and criteria by which the objectives and goals in life are measured. Their long-range future depends on these choices! It is believed by many that "direction" is given once and "guidance" often. An example would be a space rocket launched to the moon. It has a programmed direction and if it gets off course the guidance system brings it back on course in order to successfully reach the ultimate destination. The caregiver's primary task is to assist the child in knowing his or her purpose in life, and, if they get off course, provide the gentle guidance needed to get them back on track. Purpose is never plural; one cannot travel in more than one direction at the same time. Objectives, goals and standards are always plural, because they are sub-sets of the purpose.

The purpose must be divided into more than one objective and each objective must have more than one goal to assure the objective has been reached. There are multiple standards or criteria to assess when a goal has been reached. More than one goal must be reached to satisfy an objective. As each objective is reached, the purpose, or long-range direction is advanced toward the ultimate destination. This establishes a kind of "motility" which is the capability of demonstrating forward movement by independent means. In other words: the child begins to self-actualize and assume responsibility for positive behavior that moves them in the right direction. Such positive behavior must be recognized and rewarded by the care-giver to cause the time spent in custodial care to have a constructive and long-term benefit for the child.

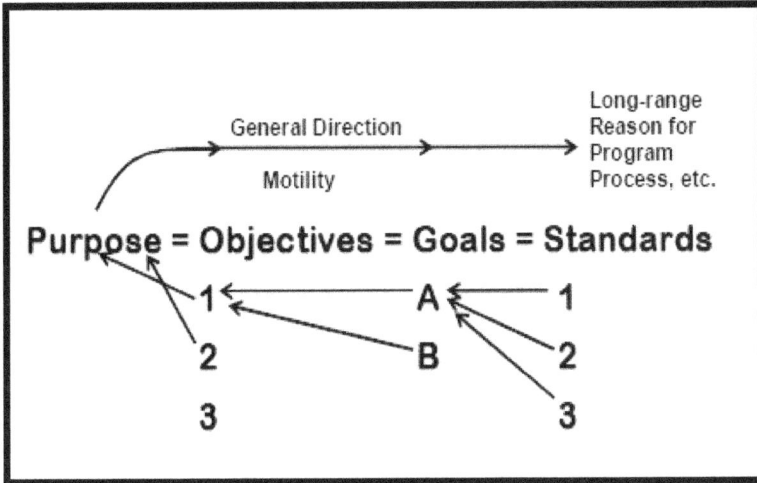

Figure 8

Philosophical Razors

The term "razor" is used for philosophical constructs that guide an individual to "scrape" away unnecessary layers of data in order to get at the vital core. When using one of the philosophical razors, an individual scrapes away various layers that cloud the ultimate understanding and/or solution of the problem. It is kind of a mental archeological dig that finds important clues from the past to inform the present.

Ockham's Razor

William of Ockham, an English logician in the 14th century, proposed a principle that stated in the explanation of any observable experience one should make as few assumptions as possible, eliminating those that make no difference in the observable outcomes. The principle is often expressed in Latin as the law of frugality or succinctness and roughly explained as "the essence of something must not be multiplied beyond necessity." This is often paraphrased as **"All other things being equal, the simplest solution is the best."** In other words, when multiple competing speculations are equal in other respects, the principle recommends selecting the assumption that introduces the fewest suppositions and proposes the fewest contradictions. It is in this sense that Ockham's Razor is usually understood; it is more often used today as a rule of thumb to encourage simple solutions to what may appear to be a complicated psychological or social mess. It is normally accepted that there are no simple solutions to the dysfunctional family; however, removing a child from an unacceptable environment is an improvement of itself. Placing that child in a place where they can receive remedial and surrogate parenting is a basic solution to the dysfunctional family.

It is in the light of Ockham's Razor that caregivers must take a simple and common sense approach to remedial development of a neglected or abused child. Do not complicate the process by negative thoughts about the process. It is not necessary to hire expensive professionals, a wholesome maternal nature with the touch of divine influence is usually sufficient. Trust your maternal and/or paternal instincts and constantly evaluate your own attitude, knowledge, and behavior in relation to the child's need and the long-term goals of custodial care.

Opportunity equals Obligation

There is a corollary principle in philosophy called Hanlon's Razor; it was simply stated, **"Do not attribute to malice what can be explained by stupidity."** Notwithstanding that stupidity, ignorance, or neglect of others may surely complicate the early life of a child, caregivers in the custodial arena should consider the opportunity to participate in the remedial development of a neglected or abused child as a divine intervention. Jesus said, "Suffer little children to come to me, of such is the Kingdom of Heaven!" When a child has been living "on the outskirts of Hades," a surrogate caregiver has an opportunity to bring the child into the arena of authentic affection and safety. One should never be indifferent or neutral when it comes to an abused or neglected child. Caregivers should count it a joy when given the opportunity to be a change agent in a child's life. In my judgment, opportunity equals obligation for intervention! This means involvement, intercession, and a deliberate entry into a situation to influence events or prevent undesirable consequences. This is what custodial care is all about.

Surrogate Caregiver Neutrality

In contrast to the popular non-directive methods of counseling for personal problems, remedial and surrogate parenting uses a directive methodology that provides guidance and mentoring similar to the function of a teacher/ student relationship. Remedial and surrogate parenting is similar in temperament to classroom guidance, spiritual mentoring, discipleship training, and a full range of ethical and moral tutoring functions. The caregiver must guide and direct the self-activity of the child and assist the child to think for themselves rather than depend on others. Neutrality means that the caregiver does not take sides in past family conflicts, express personal feelings about the child's background, or talk with others about his or her own personal struggle. Caregiver neutrality is intended to assist surrogate parents to stay focused on issues related directly to the welfare of the child rather than be concerned with the reaction of others. In some counseling sessions, the patient may lie on a couch facing away from the counselor, but in remedial and surrogate parenting, the child and the caregiver usually sit in comfortable chairs facing each other. This face-to-face position permits positive eye contact essential to good communication.

The surrogate caregiver must stimulate interest and arouse the self-activity of the children under their care until they are willing to talk about whatever comes into mind without prompting or censoring the flow of memories. The objective is to assist the child to reach an emotional state to regress and talk about the recurrent patterns of conflict in the previous environment. Listening to children provides raw data for the caregiver to use in moving forward with the positive development of the child during discussion sessions. Nothing can replace the personal interaction between caregiver and child. The process assists with the bonding necessary to rebuild a sense of participation and partnership with positive adult contact. This is what overrides the bad memories and replaces the negative conditioning of the previous environment.

Healing Alliance and Transference

Transference is the term used for a child's repetition of previous ways of relating that were learned in an earlier environment. If the healing alliance between caregiver and child has been established, the child will begin to transfer thoughts and feelings connected with parents, siblings, or other individuals in the previous environment to the caregiver. Discussing the information gained from transference assists the child in gaining insight into the ways in which he or she misread others in the previous environment or misperceives others in the custodial environment. This is a necessary step in remedial and surrogate parenting.

At first the caregiver needs to be silent to encourage the child's spontaneous, uncensored expressions about the behavior of others in the previous environment. However, the caregiver must offer timely and sensible explanations about the information gained in child/caregiver sessions. One does not excuse previous bad behavior, but it is helpful for a child to attribute bad behavior of others to their personal weakness rather than a personal fault. Poverty, lack of parenting skills, sickness, and/or over crowded-ness, are good explanations for the weakness that caused the bad behavior of others. A child must never be permit-ted to blame themselves for the previous mistreatment. A child must clearly understand that the "fault" was in others and in the circumstances, rather than personal behavior. Once this is established, a positive break from the past environment may be facilitated and an optimistic feeling generated about the present custodial care surroundings. This step is necessary to proceed with constructive custo-dial care.

The caregiver should also use discussion sessions to uncover a child's resistance to custodial care, to dis-cuss the child's feelings about change, or to confront the inconsistencies in the child's memory. Discussions may be either focused on present issues related to changes or used to draw connections between the past and the present relative to the surroundings of the child. A child's description of dreams or fantasies may also be a source of information for the caregiver and material for discussion.

Working through the Past

After listening and discussion sessions have provided sufficient background and the child has begun to acquire insights into the real nature of present problems, working through a negative past to a positive present occupies most of the work of a caregiver. Working through is a process in which the child's new awareness is repeatedly tested in other areas of custodial life. It allows the child to understand the influence of the past on the present situa-tion, to accept it emotionally as well as intellectually, and to use the new understanding to make changes in both thinking and behavior. Working through assists the child to gain a measure of control over inner conflicts and to resolve them or minimize their negative influence. This is a necessary step.

Note of caution: Although the encounters between caregiver and child are primarily verbal, medications are sometimes used to help stabilize a child with severe nervousness, apprehension, depression, or other mood disorders during the early days of custodial care. All medications must be dispensed with the advice and prescription of medical personnel. Malnutrition from past deficiency in diet may also contribute to poor health. This means some children may need dietary supplements to gain the normal vitality needed to function as a "child." Some cases may require assistance from a dietitian or nutrition specialist, in others, simple common sense is sufficient to supply the vitamins and nutrition the child needs.

A Primary Risk

The primary risk to the child is related to the emotional stress resulting from new insights and changes in long-standing behavior patterns. In some children, custodial care produces so much anxiety that they must have more advanced professional care. In other cases the caretaker's lack of skill or even a difference in cultural background may prevent the formation of a good caregiver/child alliance. In such cases, a new caseworker or caregiver should be assigned to assure adequate care. The basic objective is positive change in attitude and behavior and acceptable adjustment to custodial care of the child. The issue is not the feelings of the caregiver; the concern is the child's welfare. This same caregiver may be "perfect" for another child's needs.

Figure 9

Whom do you see? Do you see an old women or a
young girl? Look carefully until you see both.
Then you can adequately deal with the past
and the present in the life of a child.
At least you will have a different perspective.

There is a relationship between the attitude, knowledge, and behavior of caregivers in remedial and/or surrogate parenting and quality childcare.

Like footprints each child is different!

Chapter Eight

THE RELATIONSHIP CYCLE

Maturity and the Cycle

Dealing with relationships is in reality dealing with maturity or the lack thereof. Maturity is more than age, it includes experience, responsibility, reliability, wisdom, and a general readiness for life as it comes. A mature person normally functions without excuses or blame and takes responsibility for their actions, deeds, manners, and general conduct.

When one is dealing with a disadvantaged child newly arrived in a custodial care facility, normally one does not see acts or behavior of a mature person. Children and adolescents have a reason to behave immaturely especially when they are taken from their known surroundings, even if they were bad, and placed in a new environment with new people. Regardless of how badly they were treated or neglected, children love their biological family and a familiar face is usually a good thing.

Arriving in custodial care, a child will go through at least four stages: Form, Storm, Norm and Perform. In each of these stages there is a protocol for both relationship and task that must be followed to make the system work adequately. Each of these stages relate to a level of maturity, but not always age-specific maturity. This is where children must be cut some slack. Change creates conflict both physical and emotional. Make an attempt to understand the child's point of view based on background, age, present health and level of nutrition. Unless children are rested and nourished they cannot adjust well to new surroundings.

CYCLE OF RELATIONSHIP

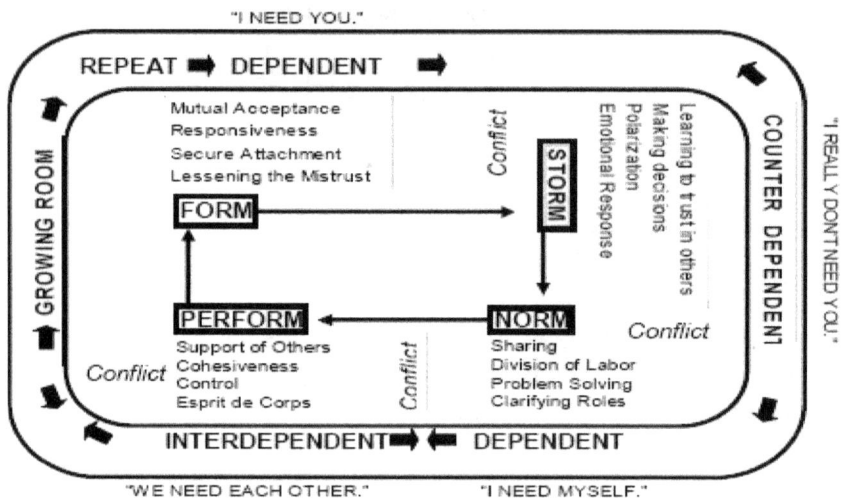

Figure 10

- Conflict occurs between each phase. No gain without pain.

- Conflict resolution is required to proceed to the next phase.

Understanding a Child's Emotional Changes

Adjustment is slow and at times painful. Moving though the stages may take five minutes, five hours, five days, or five months; no one can predict. All will go through these stages (1) Form, (2) Storm, (3) Norm, and (4) Perform in

adjusting to the custodial environment and building connections with caregivers and other residents in the facility.
It is a relational process. The behavior of the caregiver
changes as the child goes through the stages: Caregiver
first stage behavior (1) Telling (High Task/low relationship).
Normally, one would think the obvious would be High
Relationship/low task, but providing an agenda, things
to "do" simple activities, such as drinking, eating, finding
the place they will sleep, and introducing them to other
children is a good way to transition the child into the new
surroundings.

Children are smart, if you pay too much personal attention to the newcomer, you may send the wrong message.
Remember, some children have been abused and often
"close personal encounters" come at the time of abuse.
At times this attention must be age-specific; infants need
different attention than toddlers, etc. Until the caregiver
knows and understands the new child, it is best to be busy
"doing things" instead of just face-to-face talking. When a
child is in stage one emotion, they are helpless (dependent); the caregiver must "tell" them all the things they
need to know so they can begin to feel the first stage emotion of (1) **"I need you."**

The range of emotions in the child will be: **(1) "I Need
You!" (2) "I Really Don't Need You." (3) "I Need Myself."
(4) "We Need Each Other."** If one identified the stages
above as 1, 2, 3, and 4, the response attitude of the child
is (1) Form Stage -- Dependent, "I need you!" (2) Storm
Stage -- Counter-dependent, "I really don't need you."
(3) Norm Stage -- Independent, "I need myself." and (4)
Perform Stage -- Interdependent "We need each other!"
Naturally, stage four is the goal, but the emotional roller-
coaster ride and relationship cycle must pass through the
other stages as well. Knowing exactly the stage of the
child at a given time is required for the caregiver to carefully choose the behavior:

1. **Telling** (High task/low relationship),

2. **Selling** (High Task/High Relationship,

3. **Participating** (High Relationship/low task), or

4. **Delegating** (low relationship/low task).

Relationship

High Relationship High Task	High Relationship Low Task
Selling	Participating
← Leader's Behavior Telling	Delegating
High Task Low Relationship	Low Task Low Relationship

Task

FORM	STORM	NORM	PERFORM
M1	M2	M3	M4

IMMATURE ————————————————→ MATURE

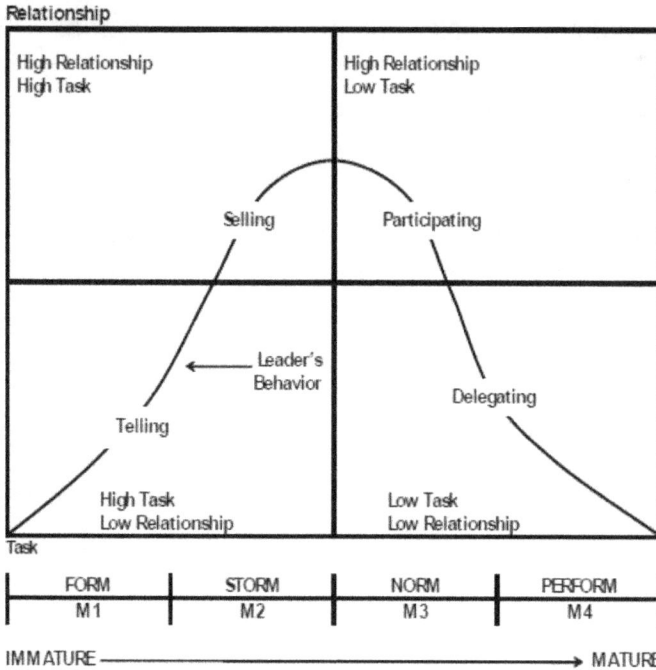

A Caregiver's behavior follows the bell curve

Figure 11

The lead caregiver's behavior is traced by the bell curve, it moves from Telling, to Selling, to Participating, and finally to Delegating. These are responses to the child's level of maturity at a given time and place. A closer review of the stages will improve an understanding of the process.

Stages of Relationship Building

Understanding the stages of relationship will assist the caregiver in friendship building with a positive outcome.

Relational and individual dynamics are prerequisite to effective relationship building with a child in custodial care. Although the Cycle of Relationship chart primarily is about a more formal relationship building process, developing a growing friendship with a child is similar and one can learn from the chart. The process does not always go forward. Certain events or changes can cause a child in the Norm or Perform stage to reset to Storm stage. It is difficult to know all the things that create this plunge backward, but it happens. When it does, the caregiver must go back to Form stage behavior (Telling -- High Task/low relationship) and move through the process again slowly.

Form Stage is the **dependent phase** for a child in the custodial relationship. There must be a mutual acceptance on the part of both the caregiver and the child for the Form Stage to begin. The objective is a mutual responsiveness. At this point the caregiver must establish rapport and find a point of secure attachment. This normally requires a conversation topic or activity that is of interest to the child. During this stage the caregiver is "telling" the child all the things that will lessen his or her mistrust of the new environment. The caregiver must be seen as an affectionate benefactor to create the **"I need you"** response which demonstrates that the child has accepted the first step in integration into custodial care. Hopefully, this "I need you" stage will last a while, but one never knows. It may last five minutes or five hours, then all the garbage breaks loose and the child goes into **Storm Stage**.

Storm Stage is a **counter-dependent phase**. The child is not sure the new environment and relationships will be beneficial. The dependent attitude was expressed as "I need you!" now the child feels **"I really don't need you"** and expresses this attitude through emotional crying or pitching a fit. This is an emotional response and the caregiver's behavior must be both kind and gentle, but always High Relationship and High Task. In other words, the caregiver must talk to the child and say things the child needs to hear. The child is responding out of a lack of knowledge and interpersonal conflict; the caregiver must respond with affection and concern. The caregiver must recognize the Storm Stage and respond to the needs of the child: does the child need food, clothing, affection, etc. The child does not need discipline at this point. The child's behavior requires the caregiver to add to the "telling" a kind of **"selling"** with the sharing of some good news and deciding on something to **"do"** quickly that can get the child's attention away from the feeling of rage or abstract disappointment.

The child has moved to the counter-dependent stage and the caregiver must "sell" the positive benefits of the new relationship by saying and doing things with the child. If the child accepts the approach, makes a decision to permit the interaction, and the emotional response is properly answered, the interaction becomes more normal. However, the child is vulnerable and remains unstable, so the caregiver must remain attentive and continue a conversation or at least talking to the child. At this point it may be best to permit the child to regress to Form Stage with the response attitude of **"I need you!"** rather than moving on to the Norm sage. At least this buys some time and provides a season of peace and rest.

It may take days or months to reach the **Norm Stage,** do not rush the process. **Norm Stage** is a participating phase, a time when caregiver and child can journey together in an agreed upon direction, doing things that mutually benefit the relationship. This is where the child begins to mature into a real person, thinking for themselves and initiating activities in which they feel totally comfortable. Actually an independent relationship develops when the child's attitude is "I need myself;" this is progress. A caregiver must not see it as a negative phase or rebellion against custodial authority; it is a natural part of developing.

During this period of walking together, the caregiver "participates" in the life and activities of the child as permitted or walks along and shares the journey without intrusion or direction. This mode is a ministry of presence and participation as the child permits; it is a good place to be in custodial care. This, of course, is done in many different ways. An appropriate way forward must be selected from several options. To maintain the norm stage, the child's larger group relationship and the custodial program of development must be considered and dealt with in a positive way. Individuals do not give up longstanding friends for a new connection that is not yet proven to be beneficial. This stage requires problem solving, clarifying of roles, and positive sharing to move to a respondent attitude of **"We need each other."** Overall, little can be done about the child's development and growth until they come to possess the "We need each other" disposition. This is the Perform Stage.

Perform Stage is an **interdependent phase** where the obvious attitude is "We need each other." When this occurs the relationship is cemented and can grow as both parties are supported. An esprit de corps develops with the new friendships. This is a kind of "can do" spirit, a sense of pride expressed in common interest and activities. When this occurs, the relationship has moved into the interdependent phase and needs additional effort to maintain. Normally, the child is delegated to handle more personal care, to dress, to make up the bed, to clean personal space, to become more involved in custodial learning activities, and more active in caregiver sessions. This is a constructive phase, but most likely will not last. Something will happen, or someone will unknowingly do something that triggers a retreat to the Storm Stage behavior of "I really don't need you" and an attitude of counter dependence.

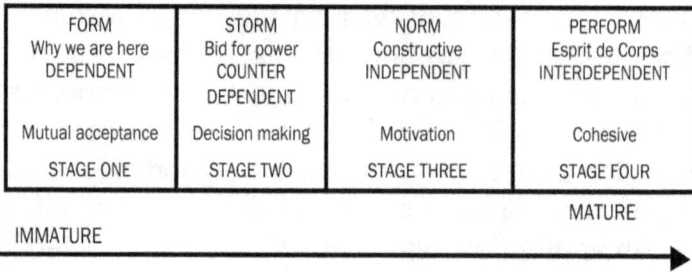

FORM Why we are here DEPENDENT	STORM Bid for power COUNTER DEPENDENT	NORM Constructive INDEPENDENT	PERFORM Esprit de Corps INTERDEPENDENT
Mutual acceptance	Decision making	Motivation	Cohesive
STAGE ONE	STAGE TWO	STAGE THREE	STAGE FOUR

MATURE

IMMATURE

$\longrightarrow$

Figure 12

Stages of Emotional Maturity

Previously it was stated that a stage could last five minutes, five hours, five days, or perhaps five months. In fact, a more realistic overview of this cycle of relationships as it relates to custodial care is an overall time frame of about 20 months from the time a child enters the facility until they reach a firm and stable place in the Perform Stage. There will be many ups and downs depending on the age-level maturity of the child. There will be areas of life, certain activities, and relationships with certain individuals that the child's show of maturity will be different. Caregivers must be aware of different emotional reactions to different people and circumstance. But a realistic timetable would be for the child to spend about five (5) months in each of these stages. That does not mean that the child will not move beyond the form level in relation to many events, occasions, and with certain people; it means the stable emotional stage will be placed in the Form Stage for about five months before it can be moved forward. Even then it will reset to a place of comfort. This is dealing with the overall maturity of the child and total adjustment to custodial care.

There will be time, places, and with certain people that the child demonstrates different levels of maturity. In other words, the child may develop a different timetable for each activity, event, occasion, or person. In actuality the child may go through the form/storm/norm/perform cycle many times on many different occasions with different activities. It is the long-term timetable for adjustment to the custodial care facility that could take up to twenty (20) months with set-backs occurring at different times under different conditions with different activities, programs, or people. Be patient. Rome was not built in a day. It took the Creator six days to make the universe and then even the Creator took a day of rest!

When this process is understood, a caregiver can adequately integrate most children into custodial care. Building a relationship with a child is the steady influence of a friend who reasons with facts to solicit a positive attitude. This process includes winning the child over and convincing the child of the benefits of the new surroundings. One cannot set a time frame for the stages of relationship building. It takes maturity and wisdom to make it work. The facts are that a caregiver may start each day with a child or with each activity at square one or the Form Stage. If so, simply go through the steps in the process of behaviors one at a time until the child is at the desired level for each occasion.

An observant caregiver can see the various emotional stages of the child moving from dependent,(I need you) to counterdependent, (I really don't need you) to independent, (I need myself) to interdependent (We need each other). In other words, these stages are not static. They are emotional stages similar to finding where pieces fit into a puzzle or points on a compass that the least variation in magnetism can cause the needle to point in a different direction. When one is dealing with a disadvantaged child in a new and different environment surrounded by children who are not their siblings and adults who are not their kinfolk, one can see the volatile nature of the atmosphere. Relationship building with a child cannot be just "telling," one must get inside the mind and heart of the child and understand their plight and reluctance to participate. To the greater degree a caregiver understands the Form – Storm – Norm - Perform process and the more they appreciate the child's circumstances, the more effective they will become in dealing with the child and the greater the personal and professional satisfaction they will receive from their service in the custodial arena.

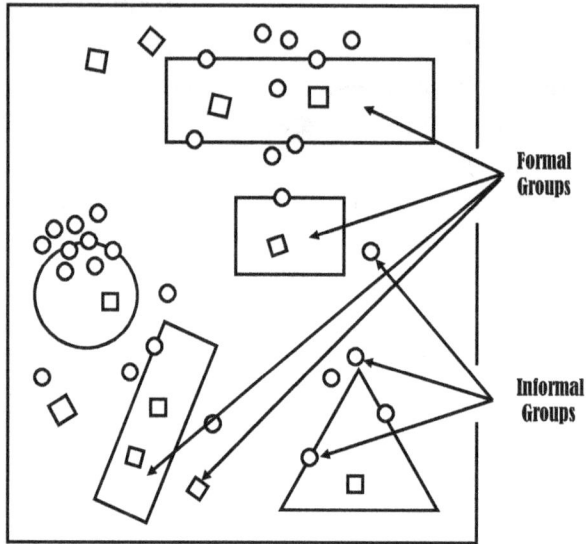

The Maze of Custodial Care Activities and Programming

Figure 13

As new children entry a custodial care facility, they see many new and strange things that make them uncomfortable. This maze and hub of activity can overwhelm a new child, especially those who have been left alone. They see a locked gate, a closed door, and unfamiliar adults standing around. At this point they do not and cannot see a way out or a way through this place. A change of residence is traumatic for a child, especially when all the familiar faces are missing and replaced with strangers. A child who existed in inadequate accommodations with limited activities and few contacts with strangers will be apprehensive. It is the caregiver's responsibility, no it is the caregiver's opportunity, to lead the child through the custodial maze and remove the fear and apprehension of new things. The new environment should be an exciting place filled with pleasant things, happy people, good food, playing children, friendly adults, and an affectionate and caring atmosphere.

The basic objective of the caregiver is take a sad and disadvantaged child and lead them through the strategic maze of custodial care until they emerge into the real world as a happy and productive individual with sufficient grace and moral fiber to raise and support a family and be a productive member of society. This will take time, but the outcome is worth the investment of energy and resources.

Figure 14

The ultimate objective is to lead the child to a joyful exit of the facility at the proper time and in the proper manner so that there will be a good feeling about the place as they face the hostile world. When an alumnus of a custodial care facility feels a sense of appreciation and a willingness to support the facility with future resources, the job was well done. In order to facilitate this positive and ongoing relationship, each caregiver and each custodial care facility must maintain contact and a supportive connection with all the children that are processed through the facility. Surrogate parenting must continue to be a part of the individual life, career, and family of all who exit the facility.

In other words, the caregivers and the facility have a stake in all the alumni of custodial care. This is part of the follow-up care that is needed to counteract the loss of family relationships. Also, it may be necessary to prevent negative influences that may come from blood relatives and family associates who caused a big part of the problem in the first place. This must not happen. *Find a way to keep in touch!*

Like footprints each child is different!

CHAPTER NINE

A CHILD AND DEVELOPMENTAL GROWTH

Parents and surrogate caregivers must be patient! Growth and development take time; they often go in spurts of growth and inactivity. Nature has taught us that it takes months from conception to the birth of a child. And from infancy to toddlerhood, to adolescence, to the teenager, and adulthood there are particular spaces of time and incremental developmental phases. The same will be true in the growth and development of children in custodial care.

An Ongoing Project

When the early spiritual awakening came to the city of Antioch and Barnabas needed assistance in disciplining and training the young, Saul of Tarsus was invited to come to the city and assist with the nurturing and instruction of the new ones. Sacred writing was clear that after one whole year of discipline and training the young became similar to their teachers in attitude and behavior and were identified as becoming akin to the Master Teacher. Caregivers may not be fortunate enough to have the assistance directly of the Master Teacher from the past, but they do have the concepts, constructs, and sacred writings left behind to assist with faith-based instructions. Still custodial caregivers may not be able to guide all the children in their care to become moral and ethical adults, but they will improve, develop, and they will grow. Each individual child and society as a whole will be better for the effort of dedicated caregivers.

Lessons about Growth

Nature also teaches us growth lessons by observing the growth of a tree. It seems that a child grows much as a tree grows. There are two kinds of trees: deciduous and coniferous trees. A deciduous tree is seasonal in its spurts of growth and dormancy. A deciduous tree is normally inactive or dormant to survive adverse environmental conditions. While a coniferous tree, often called an evergreen, continues to grow all year long and makes incremental changes consistent with their growth. Children are similar, some grow and develop in spurts while other become inactive for short periods of time, still others constantly grow and develop incrementally as an evergreen. Hopefully, each caregiver understands and works with both kinds of growth and sees both the seasonal and the constant growth as a natural occurrence and a marvel of human nature.

A child is similar to a tree planted by the water that will ultimately bring forth fruit, but first it must grow. A tree grows in four areas: the root system, the trunk and branches, and the foliage and fruit bearing area. A tree is as large in the root system as it is above ground and so is a child. The background of the child directly impacts the size and quality of the child. A child must be given room to grow.

A tree grows in the root system, which is the supply or nourishing aspect of the tree although the leaves do assist with the acquisition of oxygen and water vapor. Trees also grow just beneath the bark in the trunk and branches in a support system that provides strength and stability to the tree. Then there is growth in the terminal bud of each limb where the foliage and fruit bearing system begins. It should be noted that fruit does not grow on the roots, branches, or even the terminal bud: fruit is only on new growth. However, the other aspects of growth are required or there will be no fruit.

A Kind of Horticulturist

A surrogate caregiver is a kind of horticulturist planting and nourishing a child to grow and develop in several areas of life. The cultivator of plants, especially flowers, fruit, and vegetables in gardens and greenhouses using a simple form of agriculture based on working with small plots without using animals or plows is called a horticulturist. Caregivers in this simple role nourishing a child must furnish a healthy supply system to foster growth together with additional fresh air and stream of sustenance from the extended family within the custodial arena. The support system must develop, not only in the principle structure of the child, but in the auxiliary areas of bonding, personality, knowledge, character, and spiritual formation. Only when all of the complex elements of growth and development work together will the child's life become fruitful and the child a future productive member of society.

Caregivers Must Find Common Ground

Progress for children in a custodial environment may require the mixing of traditions and cultures. By adding some aspect of one culture to another, the assimilation produces common ground. The combination of traditions produces transformation and adjustments to both thought and process. As change is assimilated, answers are worked out in advance of anticipated questions and a positive attitude for interaction becomes an active policy for child development. This tactic produces a strategy for positive change as children adjust to the differences around them. The ability to accommodate and adjust to a new environment or a larger association is a noble and valued aspect of human nature. In fact, this is what makes the world go around or at least move forward toward common ground known as social progress. Where cultures and traditions overlap becomes common ground.

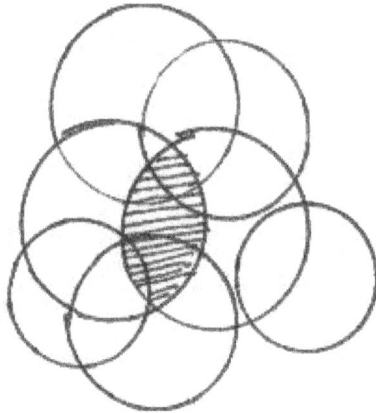

Cultural Overlap Creates Common Ground

Figure 15

There are many approaches to child development and care. As individuals function within a given culture or tradition, they constantly seek both intellectual and personal change. There is an automatic reaching for a new and different way; an ambitious striving toward different and higher goals. Of course, there are restraining forces that obstruct such progress. raints that prevent progress come in the forms of persons, traditions, and certain aspects of culture: food, clothing, music, religion, politics, and personal and social distance. As one matures, one becomes willing to overlook traditional and cultural warnings and traverse or navigate and at times negotiate both social and personal distance to better understand those around them. It is this course of action that facilitates positive growth and child development in the custodial arena.

In a pluralistic environment there is concern that one does not become tainted by the moral deficiencies of another culture, tradition or individual behavior. One must be vigilant, willing to take a cautious look at other cultures and traditions, but also be discerning and accept only those aspects of culture or tradition that do not violate one's moral standard. The intention is to allow good to overcome evil rather than to sanction immoral behavior. Should one accept the dishonorable aspects of a culture or tradition and attempt to imitate shameful behavior, a progressive debauchery establishes a slippery slope toward wrong doing that produces deterioration and decline in the moral values and meaningful traditions of the community.

Everyone must be on guard against moral decline that ultimately harms the family and children. The process of integrating disadvantaged children to a custodial care facility, however, is designed to make the child whole or new by adding or bringing together different people and programs to do remedial work on the child's problems. The study of faith-based information and/or philosophy creates one's value system and ideology. At the level of ideology and values, different individuals and divergent groups find common ground to effect cooperation. This takes place as a formation in the affective domain where ideas of an individual or class are derived exclusively through feelings.

Since feelings can be deceptive, the affective domain must be balanced with a basic philosophy by learning about the processes governing thought and conduct including aesthetics, ethics, logic, metaphysics, morals, character and behavior. This should be combined with a morsel of faith-based thinking that considers the relationship between the Creator and the universe as to matters of faith and behavior.

Why do morality and ethics have difficulty in a pluralistic environment? What is the inferior process that weakens the moral fiber? Why has the message of mercy and forgiveness failed to be a viable expression of morality to the children in a dysfunctional family? To do remedial and surrogate parenting in a pluralistic environment and guide children in the area of moral values, caregivers must have a comprehensive grasp of the many aspects of culture and tradition. Also, these must be faced with an open mind and a willing heart.

Short-Interval Assessment

In business, a technique called short-interval scheduling is used to make certain all the elements of a production line are completed in a timely manner and that the finished product is complete in all respects. Caregivers must do some short-interval assessment of the basic areas of child development to be certain that all elements are progressing in time and together. According to ancient writings, the boy Jesus grew in (1) wisdom, (2) statue, (3) favor with God, and (4) favor with man. This was development in four basic areas: mental, physical, character/spiritual, and social. Most authorities affirm that all children need to develop in these areas and in this sequence. That is, a certain mental or cognitive development begins in the womb and continues rapidly after birth. After the crisis of birth, physical growth takes hold and the child grows physically in a visible manner. What is not easily observable is the incremental elements of character development or small bits of spiritual formation that takes place as a child develops naturally. Then there comes the big step of social relationships and the development called socialization.

Provided one constructed a parallelogram, a rect-
angle with non-equal sides, and placed mental / physical
/ spiritual / social on the four sides, it would be easy to
see that the physical and social are longer and the mental
and spiritual are shorter. In short-interval assessment, the
caregiver must see that the physical and social elements
appear to be much larger in quantity, and the mental and
character/spiritual aspects, although not easily observed,
must also be developed if one is to witness the maturing of
a normal child into adolescence.

PHYSICAL

MENTAL | **SHORT-INTERVAL ASSESSMENT OF CHILD DEVELOPMENT** | **SPIRITUALITY**

SOCIALIZATION

Figure 16

All of these should be observed, assessed, and evaluated regularly. If the four sides are not proportionally developed there must be more emphasis and guidance in
the weak areas. Beware that children develop physically
and socially with ease while mental development and the
emotional aspects of life that build character and construct
a spiritual foundation require more work.

Caregivers must be advised that the elements of character; such as, temperament, disposition, moral fiber, integrity, and reputation develop slowly over time. Spirituality
and bits of spiritual formation are slow to develop, although

they can be recognized even in small children who have been exposed to affection, music, nature, and worship. The quality or condition of being spiritual and the ability to connect higher-level emotions by mind, spirit and temperament to the sacred is the beginning of spirituality. There is a significant difference between character and spirituality, and between religion and faith-based orientation. Character is related to moral fiber and the showing of refinement and concern for the better things in life, spirituality is more emotional and mystical and religion is more codified adherence to teachings; while faith-based orientation is belief in a Divine Creator, legal justice, social fairness, and human equality. This comes when one understands that the Creator made "of one blood all nations." Hopefully, a faith-based lifestyle would lead ultimately to a personal acknowledgment of need for salvation. All caregivers may be able to do is plant the good seeds of faith and honesty and permit the tree to grow and flourish into adulthood.

All Growth Follows an S-curve

All growth, a human infant, an elephant, a tree, or even social entities such as the stock market, grow and develop in a clear S-curve. An understanding of the S-curve of growth that the life of all organisms and organizations demonstrate is essential to those who would adequately care for children. The S-curve of growth has three phases: a period called the lag phase (I) when preparation and a framework is being made for growth. The period of actual growth is called exponential or logarithmic phase (II). This period of rapid growth and development climaxes in maximum efficiency and usually gives way to a healthy development through a constructive coordination of differing facets of the individual into a uniform whole. At this point in development a stationary phase (III) usually develops because of the effort of the individual to survive and maintain basic identity. When the crisis is not met, the energies and resources normally used for growth and development are re-channeled to maintain status quo; thus, the leveling off period is entered, when growth ceases and development stabilizes. This is usually called the stationary phase and is the most critical. (See Figure below)

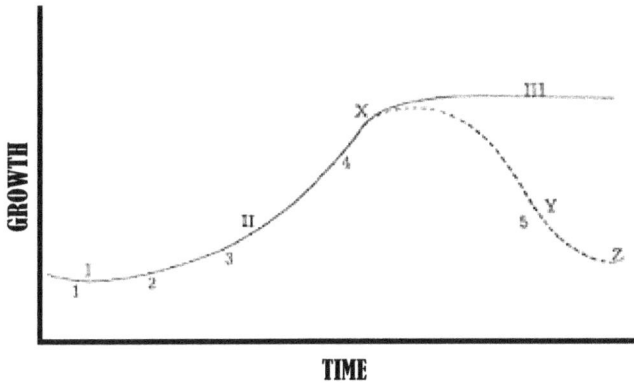

Figure 17

Diagram of the normal growth curve above is for all growth: I-lag phase, II-logarithmic phase, III-stationary phase, X-point of crisis. The Y represents decreased development and the Z points to fixed development below potential. The third stage is a stationary period where development appears to stop or level off. This is the point of crisis and caregivers must maintain high relationship and high task to move the child forward. After a child reaches departure status (time or age) the Y and Z may be beyond the domain of the caregiver. This is why caregivers must use all the time available to give the child quality care and plant the seeds of achievement for the future. Ancient sacred writings made it clear that a child who was "trained" properly would maintain an awareness of early instructions even as they grow older.

All growing entities have a lag phase early in life when it seems they are not growing. Then a logarithmic phase of rapid growth begins that may appear to be exponential. Numbers 1-5 are the normal stages of human development: (1) a weak entry into the real world from the womb, (2) a formal structure and routine for life is established, (3) a period of mental, physical, spiritual and social growth happens, (4) a more formal developmental stage becomes obvious, and (5) if one is not careful there will be a disintegration of concepts and constructs that brought about growth and development as the individual reverts to previous habits and routines. This is the real difficulty in custodial care and causes most of the failures. Do not be disturbed by this normal process. Keep the following prayer always in your mind.

Lord, help me to remember that
nothing will happen to me today that
you and I together can't handle!

General Discussion Questions

1. What role does common sense play in childcare and development?

2. Could inherited traits and genes explain a child's bad behavior?

3. What about the previous environment and the limitation of care by a nuclear or extended family?

4. Does the normal response to external stimuli (environment) explain a child's behavior?

5. How does personal or internal motivation affect child performance?

6. Where do selfish actions and/or aggressive behavior originate?

7. Does a caregiver have the potential to undo or override the past negative programming of a child and thus affect a more productive future?

8. Do children have control over the acts that determine their future? If not, who does?

9. What about the impact of spiritual formation and caregiver intervention on child development?

10. How long does it take to turn a child around after a bad environment?

11. What is remedial and surrogate parenting?

12. What is a custodial facility and what is its purpose?

APPENDICES

A

POSITIVE TECHNIQUES FOR GUIDING CHILDREN

B

GUIDELINES FOR A VOCATIONAL DIRECTION

C

YOUTH MONEY MANAGEMENT

D

AMERICAN ACADEMY OF PEDIATRICS

E

STAGES OF MORAL DEVELOPMENT

APPENDIX A

Positive Techniques for Guiding Children

— to avoid punishment, hurt feelings, and developmental setbacks

—Adapted from <u>Memos from Mims</u>, by Helen G. Morgan, PhD, and used by permission. <u>Memos from Mims</u> is a paper providing the positive guidance of an affectionate grandmother, known to her grandchildren as "Mims", to summarize her years of work as a professor concerned with childcare and early childhood education.

l. Know developmental and age-specific needs for children under your care. If you know the needs they have, you are more likely to plan activities that will meet those needs.

2. Planning prevents problems. Plan ahead the activities that will meet needs of the child or children. Plan schedules that provide variety and let children know what to expect in the day's activities. Knowing what is expected at certain times helps them feel comfortable.

3. Tone of voice is a major key to being loving and accepted by children. Tone of voice indicates that you are in a good or bad mood, or if you are happy or sad, and if you are a pleasant person or a grouch. Children automatically know which kind of person they prefer to be around.

4. Feel positive about yourself. Present yourself to children in a loving and caring way, a person who will help them to learn and enjoy the daily routines.

5. Get down on the level of the child to communicate. Sit on the floor or in a low chair with them. Cuddle them close to you if necessary to see their eyes and know they are hearing you. Soft tones will be more effective than yelling which may cause fear in children. Fear should never be used as a guidance technique. It has the opposite effect you desire even if you get an obedient response.

6. Give clear instructions to the child, telling them what to do instead of what not to do. Using the phrase "it is time to", or "you need to" carries much weight in getting the child to follow directions.

7. Avoid saying "NO" unless it is a matter of caution that could lead to an emergency. (such as their running toward the street). The fact that using NO is overdone in most families has made it unacceptable.

8. Redirect a child's unwanted behavior by suggesting an activity that will still give consideration to the interest of the child.

9. Choose age-specific activities that successfully promote a good self-concept. A task that is too advanced for the child means he will become frustrated and feel unsuccessful. You want children to feel that they can, not that they cannot complete a task.

10. Always be generous with praise when a child is successful, whether it be in physical development (as in learning to skip) or in a play activity (working a puzzle), or in social development (as when a child shares.) If a child is having problems in some area of development, you can plan activities at which the child can succeed and praise generously when the child is successful.

11. Don't compare children. Remember the value of individuality and remember that children have individual rates of development. Try not to develop within the child a feeling that all must be alike to be successful. Teach the value of having differences.

12. Be aware of all four kinds of development: mental, physical, emotional and social. You must plan activities that will contribute to all areas of child development. Review regularly what tasks children should accomplish at each age. Know the general process of development, from head to toe, and from center outward. Vary active time and quiet time. Plan for individual free-play and also time for group play.

13. Choose words carefully when giving instructions. Telling the child what to do, not what not to do or following with threats of what will happen if the instructions are not followed. Threatening a child promotes fear and destroys trust. An infant develops trust just from having physical needs cared for by a gentle and kind caregiver. To change, feed, rock and cuddle an infant promotes the feeling that the infant is somewhere that he or she can count on being cared for by a kind and loving person.

14. Keep promises and develop a child's trust. Knowing they can depend on you is important. So keep your word! Trust is basic to the development of a religious faith and can be influenced by quality of childcare.

15. Prevention of problems is the best way to deal with problems. Be aware of what is happening at all times. Prevention may involve knowledge, good planning, as well as awareness of what is happening with children. Understanding of individual needs that require specific acts of prevention can help both the child and the caregiver be successful.

16. Avoid labeling the behavior of any child that may cause them to feel they are a loser, a problem, a failure, or negative in any way. Such labels stick in the child's mind and affect the child's self-concept. Any kind of attention that causes the child to be embarrassed or ashamed should be avoided.

17. Follow a schedule that is considerate of the child's basic needs for sleep, rest, quiet time, active time, varied physical activities and time for a snack or a meal. If a child is tired, sleepy or hungry, more difficulties may be expected. Variation is a good guide. Keep a written schedule that gives you clues as to what is working and why.

18. Use a "time out" chair to isolate a child in order to gain control when behavior has gotten out of control and is not acceptable. Time to think about the problem or simply time to "cool off" may be necessary. Spanking or paddling compounds the problem and teaches a child that fighting is the way to solve problems. Spanking a child who displeases you, gives the child an idea they may hit another child when there is a disagreement. In some places paddling may be considered an assault on a child. At best it indicates that supervision and planning were not successful in prevention of the problem for which the child was corrected.

19. The use of distraction can be a way to deal with unwanted behavior without telling the child not to do the behavior. It gives a chance for you to redirect without calling attention to the bad behavior.

20. Give the child choices only when it does not matter which way the child chooses. If it is time for a nap, don't ask "do you want to take a nap?" instead say "It is time for your nap."

21. Treat the cause and not the symptom of a child related problems. Why is the child crying? Or yelling? Is he hungry or sleepy? Is the child afraid of something or somebody? Has someone said or done something that hurt the child? Look for the cause of the behavior and explore the need for change.

22. Cultivate a peaceful attitude and atmosphere throughout the time you are caring for children. They will be happier and so will you. Singing, music, praise, and happy voices should be evident if there are happy children and caregivers around. Staying calm, using a soft tone of voice, choosing words that give comfort, and good feelings should characterize the setting, whether at home or in a childcare facility.

Guidelines for a Vocational Direction

STRONG INTEREST INVENTORY (SII)

According to Wikipedia, the free encyclopedia, the Strong Interest Inventory (SII) is a psychological test used in career assessment. It is also frequently used for educational guidance as one of the most popular personality assessment tools. The test was developed in 1927 by psychologist E.K. Strong, Jr to help people exiting the military find suitable jobs. The newly revised inventory consists of 291 items, each of which asks you to indicate your preference from three responses.

The test can typically be taken in 25 minutes after which the results must be scored by computer. It is then possible to show how certain interests compare with the interests of people successfully employed in specific occupations. Access to the comparison database and interpretation of the results usually require a fee (75USD). Institutions normally order in bulk and save. Strong Interest Inventory is a registered trademark of CPP, Inc. of Mountain View, California. The results include:

1. Scores on the level of interest on each of the six Holland Codes or General Occupational Themes.
2. Scores on 25 Basic Interest Scales (e.g. art, science, and public speaking)
3. Scores on 211 Occupational Scales which indicate the similarity between the respondent's interests and those of people working in each of the 211 occupations.

4. Scores on 4 Personal Style Scales (learning, working, leadership, and risk-taking).

5. Scores on 3 Administrative Scales used to identify test errors or unusual profiles.

FINDING A VOCATIONAL DIRECTION

Parenting or surrogate childcare is not completed until the child is prepared for adult participation in the real world of work and play. In most cases, the intention is for youth to find employment in a profession, in business or industry, seeking in those areas the best opportunities for exercising God-given abilities. Youth should be guided to demonstrate a moral and ethical life in daily work by dedication to duty, by jobs well done, and by high personal integrity.

Life's vocations should not be divided into the sacred and the secular, as though the two were independent and unrelated. Today's world offers an unlimited opportunity for dedicated moral and ethical individuals to find their service field in careers that are usually referred to as secular.

Consider becoming:

- an accountant who counts blessings;
- an advertising agent who also proclaims the "good news;"
- an artist to paint the beauty of holiness;
- a banker who is a faithful steward;
- a businessman busy doing good;
- a chemist who seeks a moral answer to life's equation;
- an engineer acquainted with divine dynamics;
- a farmer who "sows to the spirit";
- a parent who understands family priority and the value of each child;
- an insurance worker with an "eternal life" policy;

- a journalist whose best story is a personal testimony;
- a lawyer who keeps divine laws;
- a medical doctor who believes in the Great Physician;
- a nurse demonstrating the compassion of Christ;
- a salesman who is "bought with a price";
- a teacher taught by the Master Teacher;
- a technician who realizes that all knowledge is of God;
- a scientist who understands the creative force of the Divine;
- a politician who accepts divine guidance.

The first step in search of a suitable vocational objective is to obtain a panoramic view of the field. This can be done by browsing through any school or public library or through a search engine on the Internet. The librarian or a "key word search" will guide you. After you have become acquainted with a number of vocations, you can focus on the particular ones that appeal to you, the careers that seem to fit best with your objectives, your talents, your abilities, and your passion.

Each major vocational field is made up of a variety of jobs. Many types of people from professional to unskilled workers are employed in each field. The workers are held together by a company, a contract or an objective – the production of a product or service for public or private use. You may not be able to select your actual job, but you can choose the field from which your future employment will come. You can decide on a vocational direction and begin the decision process that qualifies you to participate in the chosen field.

Twinkle, twinkle, little star;
How I wonder what you are!

Why do stars twinkle? How far are they from the earth? What is their magnitude, age, size and color? The principal stars visible to the naked eye have a name. Did you know that? Have you ever wondered about them? Have you ever met a banker, an engineer, a lawyer, a missionary or an accountant? Did you ever wonder what their work was and how they lived their lives? What kind of activities do they pursue? If so, you will enjoy the next paragraphs!

Accounting -- According to the **American Institute of Accountants** "A great, unfilled demand for good accountants exists today." Would you like an occupation that takes you behind the scenes of many organizations? Do you enjoy working with numbers? Have you good judgment – an analytical mind? Then you would find an interesting and stimulating career in the field of accounting.

Advertising -- Do you enjoy people and the exciting world of business? Are you sympathetic, observant, good at detail? Do you write easily or have artistic talent? Can you concentrate and produce under pressure? Can you see adventure in selling things – soap, hairpins or cars? If so, advertising may be a good career choice.

Agriculture -- Big business has moved into the agricultural activities and only a few family farms remain. Yet few people today have as much freedom of thought and action as the farmer. Are you interested in this freedom? Do you like nature? Enjoy working outdoors? Do you have a green thumb? Like animals and working with heavy power equipment? Appreciate growing things? Would you mind milking a cow or fertilizing a garden? Could you enjoy "seed time" and "harvest"? Do you have patience, endurance and determination? Then you would be a good person for some aspect of the agricultural industry.

Architecture -- Are you a young person with talent, marked intelligence and stick-to-itiveness? Would you like to have a sense of completeness in your work? Can you draw? Would you like to add to the world's store of beauty? Do you have a grasp of dimensions? Are you able to describe, in words and sketches, buildings you have seen? Do you have a feeling of what is appropriate? Are you good at mathematics and technical subjects? Can you work under pressure? Are you able to "sell" yourself to people? Would you like to be a combination of businessman, organizer, technician, planner, economist, sociologist, surveyor, landscaper, engineer and artist? Then you should consider architectural services.

Art -- Raw talent, creative ability and good intelligence are perhaps the most important qualifications for an artist. Do you have these qualities? Do you like to "doodle," draw or paint? Do you have manual dexterity? Can you make a straight line or draw a circle? Are you accurate? Do you enjoy detail? Do you have patience and persistence? Can you take directions and see others point of view? If so, you probably have talent worth training. You may enjoy a fascinating career in some aspect of artistic services.

Aviation -- Do you enjoy travel? Do airplanes excite you? Do you want an unlimited future? Would you like a career with a growing industry? Do you enjoy efficiency and organization? Enjoy being part of a team? Want adventure? Then check on a career in aviation? Even if you do not want to fly, there are many areas of work in the field of aviation.

Business -- In a letter interview, I asked J. C. Penny, an outstanding American businessman, about how he hired people. His answer was clear: "I prefer a well-educated person provided they are willing to start at the bottom and learn the business." Pressing him for some clue to his business sense, he was asked his procedure of hiring employees. Again his answer was unambiguous: "I invite them to breakfast about an hour before my store opens, if they arrive on time, I consider hiring them; if they are late - I do not consider them for employment." Another thing I remember from that letter interview, Mr. Penny said, "I watch the person order their breakfast. If they hesitate or if they salt or pepper their food before tasting, I do not hire them." When asked why did this matter, his answer, " If they hesitate to order when they have eaten the same breakfast for years or salt or pepper food before tasting they may try to solve problems that do not even exist or not be deliberate enough for retail work. I cannot afford such workers."

Mr. Penny continued, "It is necessary to be ambitious, energetic, trustworthy and honest. (this includes dependability and reliability). One should not be afraid of work." Are you at ease with people? Do you enjoy pleasing them? Do you have managerial abilities? Are you willing to work long hours? Are you able to make plans and attain goals without supervision? Do you have initiative and independence? How's your judgment and resourcefulness? Do you like to make decisions? Are you willing to take an occasional risk? What about your ability to be on time? Do you salt and pepper your food before tasting? If not, then consider a career in business.

Chemistry -- A Proctor and Gamble chemist described a young person worthy of a career in chemistry. A young person needs "a good memory, a mathematical interest, a desire to learn the basic functions of nature, a curiosity, a quality for exactness and well-established study habits to enter the field of chemistry." Do you have these? Are you a thinker, a dreamer of new things? Do you have above average intelligence? Would you have a lifetime of constant learning? Do you have courage and patience? Are you a doer, a "practical" person, who likes the thrill of actually making something? Do you like to apply your knowledge to problem solving? Why not try a career in chemistry?

Computers -- Secretarial services were the door opener for many fields in the past , but now it is the word processing and technical programming of computer services that provides a path to multiple fields. Would you like to train for a position that can lead you into any field of work that interests you? Do you have a good personality, the ability to get along with people? Are you quick and accurate? Are you dependable and have initiative? Do you like being part of a team? Enjoy working for others? Are you loyal? Have you good judgment, personal integrity? Are you adaptable? Then training for computer services can open many fields for you.

Education -- Education and in particular teaching is a challenging, exciting, rewarding career that any young person could choose, and the satisfactions are many. Are you interested? Do you like to study? Do you have good health and strong nerves? Are you adaptable? Do you have a sense of fairness? Can you be friendly yet firm? Do you have kindness, sympathy, a sense of humor and a well-adjusted personality? Do you have a sincere belief in the value of knowledge and a genuine desire to share it with others? Do you have ability to stimulate the desire to learn in others? Do you have patience and tolerance? If you have these qualities you may plan for a career in teaching or in the broader field of education.

Engineering -- A retired General Electric engineer, Daniel J. Rundell, suggested these questions be asked those desiring to enter the engineering field. "Are you able to put your ideas into words, drawing or hardware? Can you enjoy solving mathematical problems? Are you interested in the causes and effects of nature? Do you have a real interest in basic science? Are you willing to apply your knowledge to benefit humanity? Can you release your imaginative powers? Are you able to look at problems with a blind faith that they can be solved? View a process or a machine with the feeling that it can be improved? Can you think like a child who continuously asks 'Why'?" If you have these qualities and are a person of keen observation, ingenuity and inventiveness, your field could be engineering.

Finance -- Would you like to share the triumphs, the tragedies and the intimate emergencies of people in all walks of life? Have you ever been elected to handle the "funds"? Do you inspire confidence in people? Would you like a white collar job? Are you interested in and quick at mathematical problems? Are you good at "sizing things up"? Not easily misled by false claims? If so, you might be wise to consider the field of finance as a career.

Insurance -- A prerequisite to achievement in insurance is a sincere desire to meet and serve the public and the ability to stick to the job, anywhere, anyplace, and any- time. Those interested in a career in insurance should be alert, patient, have personal sales ability and be willing to work long, hard hours. Does this fit you? Are you careful, conscientious and possess good judgment and discretion? Do you show initiative? Then try a career in insurance.

Journalism -- To achieve in journalism a person must enjoy writing and be willing to devote hours to the process. Learning to write is similar to learning to ride a bicycle or to swim. You must be involved. A certain amount of background information is virtually imperative. History, social sciences, psychology and literature are particularly helpful. Do you like these subjects? Do you enjoy writing? Can you get along with all types of people? Are you willing to "dig up a story"? Are you sympathetic and understanding? Are you curious? Do you seek adventure? Then you may fit in the field of journalism.

Law -- Do you like competition? Have you a good supply of "grey matter"? Can you speak well? Are you persuasive? Are you interested in people and their problems? Do you inspire confidence? Are you willing to work? Do you enjoy serious study? Could you read stacks of dry records to prepare a case – you might lose? Are you honest? If so, you may be suited to the demanding career of law.

Medicine -- Do you desire to be one of the most respected members of your community? Would you enjoy a career full of variety, interest, and limitless opportunity to serve humanity? Are you interested in people? Are you studious? Interested in science? Do you have courage and self confidence? Do you have strong character? Do you have sympathy and understanding that give you insight to the troubles of your friends? Have you a capacity and judgment to act decisively and effectively when the situation demands? Is your family able to finance a long period of training or the grades to obtain a scholarship? Do you have the willingness to assume a great deal of personal responsibility in making decisions? Then you might look into the field of medicine.

Military or Government Service -- Serving one's country in times of peace and war is a noble profession. No one wants war; it is never politically acceptable by the general public. War is however a necessary evil in the present world condition. Therefore, the country needs honest and trustworthy men and women to serve in the armed forces. It may not seem to be a worthy profession in the minds of many, but it is a most noble endeavor. Besides the dangers, there are many advantages. The military has provided many an individual a chance at a good education and the opportunity to learn a marketable skill that assist- ed them in a civilian career.

Ministry -- Are you a dedicated Christian? Interested in soul-winning? Are you active in your local church? Do you feel a call of God on your life? Are you absolutely, prayerfully committed to God's will? Are you clear-minded, convinced, daring, willing to reach out for the high calling in life? You must have the absolute assurance and conviction that God has called you into the spiritual service. You will also need a deep-seated love for humanity, a passion for souls, a sincere desire to help your fellowman, neat appearance, and a pleasant personality. A reasonable ability to speak and to clearly express your ideas will be helpful. A deep love of study and a passion for God's Word are necessary. Seek God's will for your life. He may guide you into a life of ministry and service.

Missions -- Do you have physical stamina? Are you emotionally stable? Are you alert intellectually? Are you willing to work in a cross-cultural environment? Do you understand that the "fields are white unto harvest"? Are you socially sensitive? Are you spiritually compelled to witness for Christ? Are you willing to give your life? **Elisabeth Elliot, family of a martyred missionary in Ecuador**, remained on the field and said, "I can have no other vocation than that of a missionary." What does it take to become a missionary: absolute dedication and complete obedience to the will of God, a love for the people and an understanding of their culture and problems and a willingness to work in spite of sweat, dirt and tears. In addition to these qualities a missionary must have the quality of steadfastness. Do you have what it takes to be a missionary? Ask God for His guidance.

Music -- In addition to a marked musical talent and an appreciation for music in general, one must possess certain qualities to adequately function in the field of music. These include a desire to be a musician more than anything else, above average intelligence, physical stamina and emotional stability. Also, a willingness to study the theory of music, patience to practice long hours and a determination to achieve is necessary for those who want to make music a career. Do you have these qualities? Are you a well-integrated person? Willing to study? Are you ambitious? Do you have a sense of time, rhythm, pitch? Interested in harmony? Can you read a score, understand musical terms? Maybe you should enter the field of music.

Nursing -- Do you have a desire to serve others? Are you reliable? Do you have sympathy and skill in caring for the sick, the helpless? Do you have energy, plus an even temper and a sunny disposition? Are you in good health? Can you control your emotions? Are you discreet? Do you appreciate neatness and system? Would you be willing to prepare for a career that would help you serve humanity, be happier in marriage and parenthood? Then consider the field of professional nursing.

Public Service -- Would you like to work for John Q. Public? Are you a young person of high caliber? Do you seek satisfaction in your work? Could you enjoy prestige in a risky business? Are you interested in politics? Would you like working for Uncle Sam? **Robert C. Byrd**, an elderly US Senator **from West Virginia**, said you will need certain aptitudes to enter public service: "A warm personality that is sincere and an inherent love of people are needed. A desire to serve together with courage to express one's convictions, together with a quality of firmness to stick by decisions. Poise and patience would be among the attributes of the ideal public servant."

Some ask, "Does a Christian belong in politics?" Christians belong anywhere God wants them.   If your politics and religion doesn't mix, something is wrong with your politics. I remember writing Byrd when he was a junior Congressman asking him about his Christian witness, **Byrd** responded that a public servant "has the best opportunity to witness for Christ because so many least expect such witnessing." He went on to say that a candle in total darkness could be seen for many miles and that "my little light shines brightly in the darkness of Washington, DC." Follow the leading of God; He may have equipped you for a moral witness in public service.

Selling or Marketing -- Are you curious to know why people buy one article and treat another with complete indifference? Do you enjoy meeting new people, traveling, learning new things every day? Have you boundless energy and steady nerves? Do you have imagination? Are you equipped with initiative and common sense? Can you cooperate with others? Do you have a natural friendliness that comes from interest in others? Then you should try a career in selling or marketing.

Service or Nonprofit -- Do you enjoy working with all kinds of people? Would you like to make a positive contribution to the welfare of the world? Can you put yourself in "the other fellow's shoes" and see his point of view? Do you have a sympathetic understanding of the needs and desires that cause others to behave as they do? Do you have emotional stability, good health, good judgment and resourcefulness? Have you the ability to work under pressure and to accept supervision? Do you have a sense of humor and a determination to do "your job"? Then, social service may well be the career for you. A social worker said "It is a real joy to see someone you have aided reach a worthwhile goal."

Science -- Do you have a hungry mind? Do you search for answers? Can you enjoy struggling with a tricky puzzle or a hard problem? Do you seek the "how" and the "why"? Do you like chemistry, physics, biology, mathematics? Do gadgets, mechanisms, mechanical or electrical devices, and instruments fascinate you? Do you like to read, study and work? Do you have an interest in scientific hobbies like amateur astronomy, photography, making model airplanes, or collecting things? If so, you should look into the field of science for a challenging and rewarding career.

It is better to be safe than sorry. Self-analysis is important. It will help you determine your vocational objective. Rate yourself (1), (2), (3), (4) and (5) in the following characteristics. Be honest with yourself, but not severe. Give yourself credit for things you can do well. Admit your weaknesses. Try to think of ways to better the areas where improvement is needed.

Analyze yourself honestly. Place the number in the parentheses, (1) is excellent, (2) is good, (3) is fair, (4) is poor and (5) is bad. Read carefully and answer correctly.

( )   Ability to make and keep friends
( )   Consideration for others
( )   Emotional stability
( )   Eyesight
( )   General intelligence
( )   Physical appearance
( )   Health
( )   Hearing
( )   Language interest and aptitude
( )   Leadership ability
( )   Mathematical interest
( )   Mechanical interest
( )   Persistency
( )   Personal hygiene
( )   Poise
( )   Procrastination
( )   Special skills

( )   Special talent

( )   Special training

( )   Thrift

Now see where you stand. Is it safe to travel in the direction of your desired vocation? (1), (2) and (3) are safe. (4) is unpromising. (5) is not good at all.

With your personal survey facts in mind, you should return to your library and investigate the vocations of special interest to you. Check to see if you have "what it takes" to be successful in that particular field. You are now equipped with sufficient information to make a proper decision.

You need to know many things about your prospective career. Make a concentrated and thorough study of all angles. Find out all you can about the work. Leave no stone unturned. Make a list of important facts before you make a definite decision. A kind of "career book" on each career that interests you would be good. Such a book should include:

- a complete definition of the career
- a historical sketch of its development
- the attractive and unattractive sides
- the education required and school courses needed
- the number of persons presently employed
- the job permanence and weekly income
- the personal qualifications needed
- the opportunities for advancement
- the aptitudes required
- a day's work, hours, surroundings, conditions, etc.
- its value to the community
- how to get started

There is no excuse for anyone being careless about the future. The libraries and the Internet are full of materials on each possible career. You have a right to hope for

satisfaction in your life's work. You can expect even en-
thusiastic enjoyment in your employment if you base your
choice on personal knowledge and the will of God.

Deciding on a career is one of the biggest and most
important tasks of your whole life. This makes the task of
"digging up all this information" worthwhile. In your choice
of a career you are not only planning your means of a live-
lihood, but your way of life – a life that can be unpleasant
and uneventful or enjoyable, attractive and rewarding.

There are certain successive steps necessary to
achieve in any enterprise. To reach a successful orbit, a
man-made satellite must be launched with sufficient force,
steered in the right direction, attain the necessary speed
and arrive at a point in space. The steps to a meaningful
career are spelled out in the word.

Study these steps carefully.

1. Check all your areas of interest.
2. Arrange an interview with a professional.
3. Read all available materials.
4. Enroll in the proper study course.
5. Endure until "qualified."
6. Reach out for success with confidence.

The ladder of success is full of splinters. However, they
are more noticeable on the way down.

It would be good to keep this in mind. Check the list
below of occupations as a starter. All interested persons
should study this list in search of an occupation that meets
their personal specifications.

NON-EXHAUSTIVE LIST OF OCCUPATIONS

Management occupations

- Administrative services managers
- Advertising, marketing, promotions, public relations and sales managers
- Computer and information systems managers
- Construction managers
- Education administrators
- Engineering and natural sciences managers
- Farmers, ranchers, and agricultural managers
- Financial managers
- Food service managers
- Funeral directors
- Human resources, training, and labor relations managers and specialists
- Industrial production managers
- Lodging managers
- Medical and health services managers
- Property, real estate, and community association managers
- Purchasing managers, buyers, and purchasing agents
- Top executives

Business and financial operations occupations

- Accountants and auditors
- Appraisers and assessors of real estate
- Budget analysts
- Claims adjusters, appraisers, examiners, and investigators
- Cost estimators
- Financial analysts and personal financial advisors
- Insurance underwriters
- Loan officers
- Management analysts
- Meeting and convention planners
- Tax examiners, collectors, and revenue agents

Computer and mathematical occupations

- Actuaries
- Computer programmers
- Computer scientists and database administrators
- Computer software engineers
- Computer support specialists and systems administrators
- Computer systems analysts
- Mathematicians
- Operations research analysts
- Statisticians

Architects, surveyors, and cartographers

- Architects, except landscape and naval
- Landscape architects
- Surveyors, cartographers, photogrammetrists, and surveying technicians
- Engineers
- Drafters and engineering technicians
- Drafters
- Engineering technicians

Life scientists

- Agricultural and food scientists
- Biological scientists
- Conservation scientists and foresters
- Medical scientists

Physical scientists

- Atmospheric scientists
- Chemists and materials scientists
- Environmental scientists and hydrologists
- Geoscientists
- Physicists and astronomers

Social scientists and related occupations

- Economists

- Market and survey researchers
- Psychologists
- Urban and regional planners
- Social scientists, other
- Science technicians

Community and social services occupations

- Counselors
- Health educators
- Probation officers and correctional treatment specialists
- Social and human service assistants
- Social workers

Legal occupations

- Judges, magistrates, and other judicial workers
- Court reporters
- Lawyers, Paralegals and legal assistants

Education, training, library, and museum occupations

- Archivists, curators, and museum technicians
- Instructional coordinators
- Librarians
- Library technicians
- Teacher assistants
- Teachers—adult literacy and remedial education
- Teachers—postsecondary
- Teachers—preschool, kindergarten, elementary, middle, and secondary
- Teachers—self-enrichment education
- Teachers—special education

Art and design occupations

- Artists and related workers
- Commercial and industrial designers
- Fashion designers
- Floral designers

- Graphic designers
- Interior designers

Entertainers and performers, sports and related occupations

- Actors, producers, and directors
- Athletes, coaches, umpires, and related workers
- Dancers and choreographers

Media and communications-related occupations

- Announcers
- Broadcast and sound engineering technicians and radio operators
- Interpreters and translators
- News analysts, reporters, and correspondents
- Photographers
- Public relations specialists
- Television, video, and motion picture camera operators and editors
- Writers and editors

Health diagnosing and treating occupations

- Audiologists
- Chiropractors
- Dentists
- Dietitians and nutritionists
- Occupational therapists
- Optometrists
- Pharmacists
- Physical therapists
- Physician assistants
- Physicians and surgeons
- Podiatrists
- Radiation therapists
- Recreational therapists
- Registered nurses
- Respiratory therapists

- Speech-language pathologists
- Veterinarians

Health technologists and technicians

- Athletic trainers
- Cardiovascular technologists and technicians
- Clinical laboratory technologists and technicians
- Dental hygienists
- Diagnostic medical sonographers
- Emergency medical technicians and paramedics
- Licensed practical and licensed vocational nurses
- Medical records and health information technicians
- Nuclear medicine technologists
- Occupational health and safety specialists and Technicians
- Opticians
- Pharmacy technicians
- Radiology technologists and technicians
- Surgical technologists
- Veterinary technologists and technicians

Healthcare support occupations

- Dental assistants
- Massage therapists
- Medical assistants
- Medical transcriptionists
- Nursing, psychiatric, and home health aides
- Occupational therapist assistants and aides
- Pharmacy aides
- Physical therapist assistants and aides

Protective service occupations

- Correctional officers
- Fire fighting occupations
- Police and detectives
- Private detectives and investigators
- Security guards and gaming surveillance officers

Food preparation and serving related occupations

- Chefs, cooks, and food preparation workers
- Food and beverage serving and related workers

Building and grounds cleaning and maintenance occupations

- Building cleaning workers
- Grounds maintenance workers
- Pest control workers

Personal care and service occupations

- Animal care and service workers
- Barbers, cosmetologists, and other personal appearance workers
- Child care workers
- Fitness workers
- Flight attendants
- Gaming services occupations
- Personal and home care aides
- Recreation workers

Sales and related occupations

- Advertising sales agents
- Cashiers
- Counter and rental clerks
- Demonstrators, product promoters, and models
- Insurance sales agents
- Real estate brokers and sales agents
- Retail salespersons
- Sales engineers
- Sales representatives, wholesale and manufacturing
- Sales worker supervisors
- Securities, commodities, and financial services sales agents
- Travel agents

Office and administrative support occupations

- Financial clerks
- Bill and account collectors
- Billing and posting clerks and machine operators
- Bookkeeping, accounting, and auditing clerks
- Payroll and timekeeping clerks
- Procurement clerks
- Bank Tellers

Information and record clerks

- Brokerage clerks
- Credit authorizers, checkers, and clerks
- Customer service representatives
- File clerks
- Hotel, motel, and resort desk clerks
- Human resources assistants, except payroll and timekeeping
- Interviewers
- Library assistants, clerical
- Order clerks
- Receptionists and information clerks
- Reservation and transportation ticket agents and travel clerks

Material recording, scheduling, dispatching, and distributing occupations

- Cargo and freight agents
- Couriers and messengers
- Dispatchers
- Meter readers, utilities
- Postal Service workers
- Production, planning, and expediting clerks
- Shipping, receiving, and traffic clerks
- Stock clerks and order fillers
- Weighers, measurers, checkers, and samplers, recordkeeping

Other office and administrative support occupations

- Communications equipment operators
- Computer operators
- Data entry and information processing workers
- Desktop publishers
- Office and administrative support worker supervisors and managers
- Office clerks, general
- Secretaries and administrative assistants

Farming, fishing, and forestry occupations

- Agricultural workers
- Fishers and fishing vessel operators
- Forest, conservation, and logging workers

Construction trades and related workers

- Boilermakers
- Brickmasons, blockmasons, and stonemasons
- Carpenters
- Carpet, floor, and tile installers and finishers
- Cement masons, concrete finishers, segmental pavers, and terrazzo workers
- Construction and building inspectors
- Construction equipment operators
- Construction laborers
- Drywall installers, ceiling tile installers
- Electricians
- Elevator installers and repairers
- Glaziers
- Hazardous materials removal workers
- Insulation workers
- Painters and paperhangers
- Pipelayers, plumbers, pipefitters, and steamfitters
- Plasterers and stucco masons
- Roofers
- Sheet metal workers
- Structural and reinforcing iron and metal workers

Installation, maintenance, and repair occupations

- Electrical and electronic equipment mechanics, installers, and repairers
- Computer, automated teller, and office machine repairers
- Electrical and electronics installers and repairers
- Electronic home entertainment equipment installers and repairers
- Radio and telecommunications equipment installers and repairers

Vehicle and mobile equipment mechanics, installers, and repairers

- Aircraft and avionics equipment mechanics and service technicians
- Automotive body and related repairers
- Automotive service technicians and mechanics
- Diesel service technicians and mechanics
- Heavy vehicle and mobile equipment service technicians and mechanics
- Small engine mechanics

Other installation, maintenance, and repair occupations

- Coin, vending, and amusement machine servicers and repairers
- Heating, air-conditioning, and refrigeration mechanics and installers
- Home appliance repairers
- Industrial machinery mechanics and maintenance workers
- Line installers and repairers
- Maintenance and repair workers, general
- Millwrights
- Precision instrument and equipment repairers

Production occupations

- Assemblers and fabricators
- Food processing occupations
- Metal workers and plastic workers
- Computer control programmers and operators
- Machine setters, operators—metal and plastic
- Machinists
- Tool and die makers
- Welding, soldering, and brazing workers

Printing occupations

- Bookbinders and bindery workers
- Prepress technicians and workers
- Printing machine operators
- Textile, apparel, and furnishings occupations
- Woodworkers

Plant and system operators

- Power plant operators, distributors, and dispatchers
- Stationary engineers and boiler operators
- Water and liquid waste treatment plant and system operators

Other production occupations

- Inspectors, testers, sorters, samplers, and weighers
- Jewelers and precious stone and metal workers
- Medical, dental, and ophthalmic laboratory technicians
- Painting and coating workers, except construction and maintenance
- Photographic process workers and processing machine operators
- Semiconductor processors

Transportation occupations

- Air traffic controllers
- Aircraft pilots and flight engineers
- Security Personnel
- Material moving occupations
- Motor vehicle operators:
- Bus drivers
- Taxi drivers and chauffeurs
- Truck drivers and driver/sales workers
- Rail transportation occupations
- Water transportation occupations

Discipline is a system of rules affecting conduct that implies instruction, correction, and training that molds, strengthens, and improves character.

APPENDIX C

YOUTH MONEY MANAGEMENT

Basic Money Management Skills

Planning for the future is essential. Learning about financial planning, banking, investment advisers, and protecting money and assets is vital to young people. Caregivers should focus on guiding youth aged 9-17 years to think beyond their direct circumstances and adopt the values that will enable them to establish a more viable economic future for themselves. This will assure a sense of self-worth, personal and community responsibility, integrity and a sense of industry. This age group must be exposed to an appreciation for and the value of money and its uses. They also need information about the principles and practices of business and economy.

When a child treats money as if it grows on trees or magically falls from the sky, caregivers and guardians must teach them the true meaning of money. The primary lesson that must be learned relates to the exchange of energy for money, and money for energy. If one has money, they may hire someone to do the work. If one has energy, they may obtain work to acquire money. Perhaps each child could learn from this exchange between father and son:

"No mon-- no fun, your son!'

"Too bad-- so sad, your dad!'

Regardless of age with a little assistance children can develop the self-confidence and personal skills needed to adequately manage money. Everyone has to deal with both energy and money. Research shows that people worry more about money than any other family or personal problem. Here are four basic concepts in the adequate handling of money.

(1) Developing self-control in spending is a basic step in cutting the cost of living. Some individuals instinctively know how to get what they want, even on a limited income. Others need more guidance in managing finances to get what they need and want.

(2) If everyone understands the financial situation,xe there will be greater cooperation. A spending plan or budget to allocate income to cover expenses is a necessary step. This is a simple concept, but a challenging task for many.

(3) Everyone must learn to live within their means (earnings) rather that adapting the false notion that good credit gives them the means to live beyond their income. As my grandfather said,

When your outgo is more than your income,

your upkeep will be your downfall.

(4) Learning to save part of one's income is the key to having enough later. This is a plan not just for a "rainy day;" it is required to avoid financial disaster.

Teaching basic money management skills to young children through savings accounts is a great way to prepare children for the real world and the reality of debt. Show children the value of money by encouraging them to save money from allowance or odd jobs. When it is "their money," they learn the lessons quickly. Here are some thoughts about "money matters" that were passed to my sons:

Money is about the future! Each and every financial transaction must be weighed with reference to expectations of forthcoming expenses. A purchase is not about the present; it always relates to the future. Is this purchase absolutely necessary? Do I have sufficient funds to make this purchase? Does it use funds that will be required for future obligations? Do I have pressing future obligations that this purchase makes impossible?

Consequently, everyone must have a contingency plan relative to money. In the case of a Bank Account, an overdraw privilege is for an emergency not a regular occurrence. It is expensive to use the banks money. For example, a $36. overdraft is 10% interest on $360 or 20% interest on $720. Such expenses rob your future. A limited "safety net" is the best solution.

Establish a savings account of $200 in your name and tie it to the account for overdraft protection. The balance in such an account should always be at least $200. The goal for such a savings is to have sufficient funds to operate one month without expected income. One cannot spend anticipated funds or live on credit. This always complicates the future.

Technically, everyone has a short fall, unexpected expenses, and emergencies. Advance planning is necessary to avert damage and loss. It would be good if you anticipated what one month of expenses could be. Consider these 10 things.

1. Mortgage or rent

2. Food and medicine

3. Utilities

4. Car expenses including anticipated trips

5. Insurance and taxes

6. Entertainment

7. Required savings

8. All income must be divided into expense and savings.

9. When funds are received deposit some in checking and some in savings.

10. Avoid any behavior or action that could cause unexpected expenses: such as, traffic tickets, overdrafts, breakage of equipment or loss or neglect of property.

All caregivers need the brochure: "A Parent's Guide to Youth Money Management," presented by the Manitoba Securities Commission.

Another guide called ***Make it Count: An Instructor's Guide to Youth Money Management*** is designed in parallel to the Parent's guide by topic but differs in format. It has actual lesson plans and black line masters for instructors to use with the outlined activities. A copy of the guide may be viewed on the web site:

www.makeitcountonline.ca.

FREE download :
http://www.makeitcountonline.ca

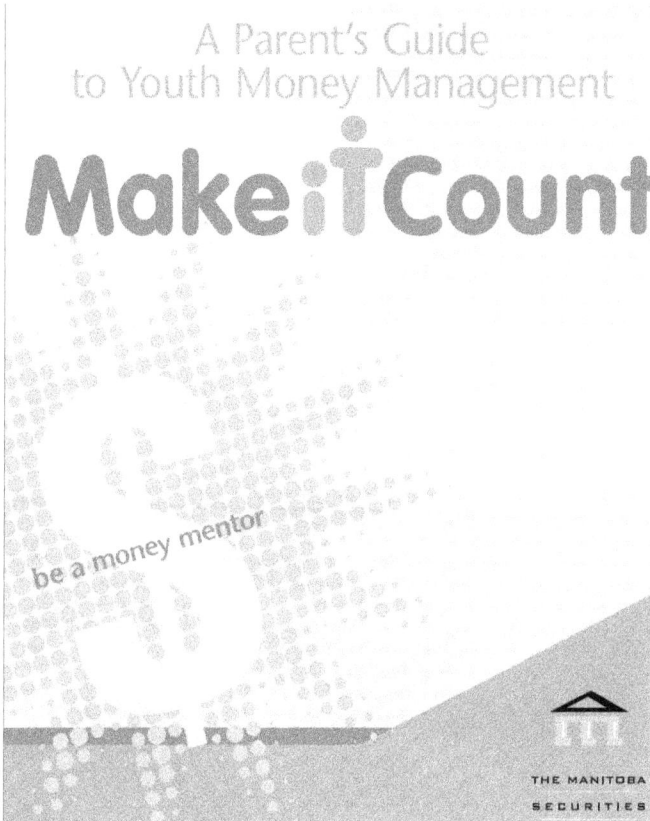

NOTES FROM THE AMERICAN ACADEMY OF PEDIATRICS

A Standard is criteria set for a certain task. It differs from a recommendation or a guideline in that it carries great incentive for universal compliance. It differs from a regulation in that compliance is not necessarily required for legal operation. It usually is legitimized or validated based on scientific or epidemiological data, or when this evidence is lacking, it represents the widely agreed upon, state-of-the-art, high-quality level of practice.

The agency, program, or health practitioner that does not meet the standard may incur disapproval or sanctions from within or outside the organization. Thus, a standard is the strongest criteria for practice set by a health organization or association. For example, many manufacturers advertise that their products meet ASTM standards as evidence to the consumer of safety, while those products that cannot meet the standards are sold without such labeling to undiscerning purchasers. In Caring for Our Children, specific standards define the frequency of visits to child care facilities and qualifications of health consultants to such facilities. Some states have adopted or even exceeded parts of these standards in their regulations, but many more have not done so. Facilities that use a health consultant, as specified in Standards 1.040 through 1.044, could be expected to be of higher quality than those that do not.

A Recommendation is a statement of practice that potentially provides a health benefit to the population served. An organization or a group of individuals with expertise or broad experience in the subject matter usually initiates it. It may originate within the group or be solicited by individuals outside the organization. A recommendation is not binding on the practitioner; that is, there is no obligation to carry it out. A statement may be issued as recommendation because it addresses a fairly new topic or issue, because scientific supporting evidence may not yet exist, or because the practice may not yet enjoy widespread acceptance by the members of the organization or by the intended audience for the recommendation.

A Guideline is a statement of advice or instruction pertaining to practice. Like a recommendation, it originates in an organization with acknowledged professional standing. Although it may be unsolicited, a guideline is developed in response to a stated request or perceived need for such advice or instruction.

A Regulation takes a previous recommendation or guideline and makes it a requirement for legal operation. A regulation originates in an agency with either governmental or official authority and has the power of law. Such authority is usually accompanied by an enforcement activity. Examples of regulations are: State regulations pertaining to health and safety requirements for caregivers and children in a licensed childcare center, and immunizations required for participation in group care. The components of the regulation, of course, will vary by topic addressed as well as by area of jurisdiction (eg, municipality or state). Because a regulation prescribes a practice that every agency or program must comply with, it usually is the minimum or the floor below which no agency or program should operate.

***

This information was taken from *Caring For Our Children National Health and Safety Performance Standards:* Guidelines for Out-of-Home Child Care Programs. Because there are no federal child care standards the American Academy of Pediatrics and the American Public Health Association have compiled their recommendations in this joint publication. *Caring for Our Children* can be ordered from the AAP Bookstore or viewed online: http://www.HealthyChildcare.org/StandardsRegulations.html

© COPYRIGHT AMERICAN ACADEMY OF PEDIATRICS, 141 Northwest Point Blvd., Elk Grove Village, IL, 60007, 847-434-4000

CHARACTERISTICS OF KOHLBERG'S STAGES

In his doctoral dissertation at the University of Chicago in 1958, and in extensive subsequent work at Harvard, Lawrence Kohlberg sought to build upon Piaget's belief that children's moral judgments shift as cognitive development progresses. In research, Kohlberg posed stories that contained a moral dilemma, then analyzed answers for evidence of different stages of moral thinking. He described six stages of moral thinking:

STAGES OF MORAL DEVELOPMENT

Age 0-2   1. Obedience and punishment orientation

To avoid breaking rules backed by punishment, obedience for its own sake, avoiding physical damage to persons and property.

Age 3-6   2. Instrumental purpose and exchange

Following rules only when it is to someone's immediate personal interest; acting to meet one's own interests and letting others do the same; right is an equal exchange, a good deal.

Age 7-10   3. Interpersonal accord and conformity

Living up to what is expected by people close to you or what people generally expect of people in your role; being good is important.

Age 11-13 4. Social accord and system maintenance

Fulfilling the actual duties to which you have agreed; laws are always to be upheld except in extreme cases where they conflict with other fixed social duties; right is also contributing to society, the group, or institution.

Age 14-16 5. Social contract, utility, individual rights

Being aware that people hold a variety of values and opinions, that most values and rules are relative to your group but should usually be upheld because they are the social contract; some non-relative values and rights like life and liberty, however, must be upheld in any society regardless of the majority opinion.

6. Universal ethical principles

Following self-chosen ethical principles; particular laws or social agreements are usually valid because they rest on such principles; when laws violate these principles, one acts in accordance with the principle; principles are universal principles of justice: the equality of human rights and respect for the dignity of human beings as individual persons; the reason for doing right is the belief, as a rational person, in the validity of universal moral principles and a sense of personal commitment to them.

* * *

1. Everybody moves through the stages in the same order.

2. Nobody skips a stage.

3. Nobody reverts to an earlier stage.

4. Different people move through the stages at different rates.

5. Not everybody moves through all the stages.

6. People are attracted to the reasoning of one stage above their position, but do not comprehend the reasoning of a stage more than one above their position.

ABOUT THE AUTHOR

Hollis L. Green, ThD, PhD, is a Clergy-Educator with public relations and business credentials and doctorates in theology, education, and philosophy. A Distinguished Professor of Education and Social Change at the graduate level for over three decades, Dr. Green is a Diplomate in the Oxford Society of Scholars, and author of 50+ books and numerous articles. He served six years as a member of the U.S. Senate Business Advisory Board and with certified membership in several public relations societies (RPRC, PRSA, and IPRC). He served pastorates in five states, was a denominational official for 18 years, and traveled in ministry and lectured in over 100 countries.

Dr. Green was the founder of Associated Institutional Developers (AID) Ltd., (1974) an international Public Relations and Corporate Consultant Company. He was Vice-President (1974-1979) Luther Rice Seminary, www.lru.edu, and became the founding President (1981) and Chancellor (1991-2008) of Oxford Graduate School,(www.ogs.edu); As part of a global outreach, Dr. Green founded OASIS UNIVERSITY (2002) in Trinidad, W.I. (www.oasisedu.org) where he continues to lecture and teach and assist the administration as Chancellor. In 2004, he assisted in establishing Greenleaf Global Educational Foundation in Colorado to advance issues related to the current needs of society.

In addition to his other endeavors, Dr. Green launched in 2007 Global Educational Advance, Inc. (www.gea-books.com) to advance higher education and social change through publishing, curriculum development, instruction, library and learning resources. The Global book distribution has 30,000 distributors in 100 countries to advance social change. His books and assisting authors in publishing are a logical outgrowth of a fifty-year ministry through education. He serves the Author Publisher Partnership PRESS as Corporate Chair and Co-publisher with his son, Barton. Dr. Green continues to travel, speak, teach, write books and work with authors in publishing.

Reviews….

Remedial and Surrogate Parenting is a well-crafted, thorough, and caring book framed by experience, critical thought, and sincere concern. The author, Dr. Hollis L. Green, has evinced tender compassion for children, and he has systematically sewn his observations to his proposed remedies in a selfless embroidery of golden aid upon today's blue social fabric. With concise, helpful insight, Dr. Green has laid problems bare, addressed today's cultural wounds, applied cleansing principles, stitched familial tears, and has bandaged broken situations through direct parallels to ancient truths that continue to shine through popular lugubriousness. If the purchaser reads Remedial and Surrogate Parenting while wearing a hat, he or she will be prompted to remove it upon the conclusion of this book. –Joshua Collins, Author and College Teacher

Remedial and Surrogate Parenting is excellent academic work providing the reader with clear and concise information on the management and care of abused and neglected children. Dr. Green's approach is comprehensive and the reader will appreciate succinct writing filled with practical ideas and strategies for behaviors the surrogate family may experience. The monograph, although useful in a classroom setting, would be a great read for the couple or individuals considering surrogate parenting or adoption of a child with an abusive/neglected developmental history. The book provides the reader with a realistic examination of what one can expect from a child raised in a compromised environment. Dr. Green does not neglect the fact that although the responsibility and commitment is great, taking a child that has yet to learn how to be loved, to love, and to form healthy relationships can be a highly rewarding and challenging endeavor. –D. Perry Timme, Jr., D.Phil., Child Counselor Farmington Municipal Schools

...the information in this book is priceless and it should be required reading for caregivers, school teachers, parents and anyone who works with children. It is the only book I have encountered that mentions history and how it affects the development of Caribbean children. I think that link is important. I especially like the layout of the book. It is easy to follow. –Stacy Ann Hansraj, UWI Tertiary Lecturer

...this book has good suggestions for caregivers and will have a broader audience than just caregivers. There is much that would contribute to the education of the workers who are not directly related to childcare. –Helen G. Morgan, PhD, Occupational Childcare Specialist and OGS Distinguished Professor of Education

REFERENCE BIBLIOGRAPHY

AACAP and David Pruitt. (1999) Your Adolescent: Emotional, Behavioral, and Cognitive Development from Early Adolescence through the Teen Years. New York: Harper Collins.

Ainsworth, M. (1978). *Patterns of attachment: A psychological study of a strange situation.* Hillsdale, N.J.: Lawrence Erlbaum Associates.

Alexander, K., Quas, J., & Goodman, G. (2002). Theoretical advances in understanding children's memory for distressing events: The role of attachment. *Developmental Review. Special issue on forensic developmental psychology,22(3).* 490-519.

Allen, Bem P. (12002) Personality Theories: Development, Growth, and Diversity. Harlow, UK: Allyn & Bacon

Anthony, E.J., & Mussen, P.H. (1970). The behavior disorders, in *Carmichael's Manual of Child Psychology.* New York: John Wiley & Sons.

Applegate, J. & Shapiro, J. (2005). *Neurobiology for Clinical Social Work.* New York: W.W. Norton & Company.

Archer, C., & Gordon, C. (2004). Parent mentoring: an innovative approach to adoption support. *Adoption & Fostering, 28(4).* 27-38.

Azmitia, E. (2001). Impact of drugs and alcohol on the brain through the life cycle: Knowledge for social workers. *Journal of Social Work Practice in the Addictions, 1(3),* 41-63.

Bakermans-Kranenburg, M., van Ijzendoorn, M., & Kroonenberg, P. (2004). Differences in attachment security between African-American and white children: Ethnicity or socio-economic status? *Infant Behavior & Development, 27(3).* 417-433.

Bandura, A. (1963). *Social learning and personality development.* New York: Holt, Rinehart, & Winston.

Berger, Elizabeth.(1999) Raising Children With Character: Parents, Trust, and the Development of Personal Integrity. Lanham, MD: Rowman & Littlefield Publishers.

Berlin, L., Y. Ziv, L. Amaya-Jackson, & M. Greenberg,(Eds.) (2005). *Enhancing early attachments: Theory, research, intervention, and policy. Duke series in child development and public policy.* New York: Guilford Press.

Bernard, C. (2002). Giving voice to experiences: parental maltreatment of black children in the context of societal racism. *Child and Family Social Work, 7.* 239-251.

Bernstein, V., Harris, E., Long, C., Iida, E., & Hans, S. (2005). Issues in the multi-cultural assessment of parent-child interaction: An exploratory study from the starting early starting smart collaboration. *Journal of Applied Developmental Psychology, 26(3).* 241-275.

Binet, A. (1896). *Alterations and personality.* New York: D. Appleton Company.

Bois, R. (2005). Parent battering and its roots in infantile trauma. In L. Greenwood,(Ed.) *Violent adolescents: Understanding the destructive impulse* (pp. 39-55). London: Karnac Books.

Bornstein, M., & Cote, L. (2004). Mothers' parenting cognitions in cultures of origin, acculturating cultures, and cultures of destination. *Child Development,75 (1).* 221-235.

Bowlby, J. (1980). *Attachment and loss.* New York: Basic Books.

Bradley, R., Corwyn, R., Pipes McAdoo, H., & García Coll, C. (2001). The home environments of children in the United States Part I: Variations by age, ethnicity, and poverty status. *Child Development, 72(6).* 1844-1867.

Brazelton, T. B., and Yogman, M. W. (Eds). (1986). *Affective development in infancy.* Westport, CT: Ablex Publishing.

Bremner, J., & Vermetten, E.(2001). Stress and development: Behavioral and biological consequences. *Development and Psychopathology. Special Issue: Stress and development: Biological and psychological consequences, 13(3), 473-489.*

Brooks, Jane. (2008). *The Process of Parenting.* 7th Ed. Boston: McGraw-Hill.

Cardona, P., Nicholson, B., & Fox, R. (2000). Parenting among Hispanic and Anglo-American mothers with young children. *Journal of Social Psychology, 140(3).* 357-365.

Chodorow, N. (1978). Mothering, object-relations, and the female oedipal configuration. *Feminist Studies, 4 (1).* 137-158.

Comer, J. P.(2002). Waiting for a Miracle: Why Schools Can't Solve Our Problems and How We Can. *Perspectives on Urban Education, 1(1).*

Cone-Wesson, B. (2005). Prenatal alcohol and cocaine exposure:

Influences on cognition, speech, language, and hearing. *Journal of Communication Disorders.* *38*(4), 279-302.

Crittenden, P. M. (1985). Social networks, quality of child rearing, and child development. *Child Development, 56 (5).* 1299-1313.

Davies, M. (2002). A few thoughts about the mind, the brain, and a child with early deprivation. *Journal of Analytical Psychology, 47(3).* 421-435.

De Bellis, M. (2001). Developmental traumatology: The psycho-biological development of maltreated children and its implications for research, treatment, and policy. *Development and Psychopathology. Special Issue: Stress and development: Biological and psychological consequences, 13(3),* 539-564.

De Bellis, M. (2005). The Psychobiology of Neglect. *Child Maltreatment.* (10) 2. 150-172.

Delaney, R. (1998). *Fostering changes: Treating attachment-dis-ordered foster children.* Oklahoma City, OK: Wood 'N' Barnes Publishing.

Dube, S.R., Anda, R.F., Whitfield, C.L., Brown, D.W., Felitti, V.J., Dong, M., & Giles, W.H. (2005). Long-term consequences of childhood sexual abuse by gender of victim. *American Journal of Preventive Medicine.* 28(5). 430-438.

English, D., Upadhyaya, M., Litrownik, A., Marshall, J., Runyan, D., Graham, J. C., & Dubowitz, H. (2005). Maltreatment's wake: The relationship of maltreatment dimensions to child outcomes. *Child Abuse & Neglect, 29 (5).* 597-619.

Erikson, E. (1959). *Identity and the lifecycle.* New York: International Universities Press.

Gardner, H. (1993). *Multiple Intelligences: The Theory in Practice.* New York: Basic Books.

Glaser, D. (2000). Child Abuse and Neglect and the Brain – A Review. *J. Child Psychology and Psychiatry. 41 (No. 1).* 97-116.

Gonzalez, V. (2001). The role of socioeconomic and sociocultural factors in language minority children's development: An ecological research view. *Bilingual Research Journal, 25 (1-2).* 1-30.

Green, Hollis L. (2008). *Interpreting an Author's Words,* Nashville: GlobalEdAdvancePress.

Green, Hollis L. (2010). *Sympathetic Leadership Cybernetics,* Nashville: GlobalEdAdvancePress.

Green, Hollis L. (2013). *Transformational Leadership in Education 2nd Ed*, Nashville: GlobalEdAdvancePress.

Green, Hollis L. (2013). *The EVERGREEN Devotional New Testament Complete Edition (EDNT)*, Nashville: GlobalEdAdvancePress.

Grych, J., Seid, M., & Fincham, F. (1992). Assessing marital conflict from the child's perspective: The children's perception of interparental conflict scale. *Child Development, 63*, 558-572.

Grych, J.H. & Fincham, F.D. (1990). Marital conflict and children's adjustment: A cognitive-contextual framework. *Psychological Bulletin, 108*(2) 267-290.

Guille, L.(2004). Men who batter and their children: An integrated review. *Aggression and Violent Behavior, 9(2).* 129-163.

Harkness, S., Raeff, C., & Super, C. (2000) Variability in the social construction of the child. *New Directions for Child and Adolescent Development, No. 87.* San Francisco, CA: Jossey-Bass.

Herbert, M.(2003). *Typical and atypical development: From conception to adolescence.* Malden, MA: Blackwell Publishing.

Holden, G. & Ritchie, K. (1991). Linking extreme marital discord, child rearing, and child behavior problems: Evidence from battered women. *Child Development, 62,* 311-327.

Honig, A. S. (2000). Cross-cultural study of infants and toddlers. In A. Comunian, & U. Gielen (Eds.), *International perspectives on human development* (pp. 275-308). Lengerich, Germany: Pabst Science Publishers.

Huang, K. Caughy, M., Genevro, J., & Miller, T. (2005). Maternal knowledge of child development and quality of parenting among White, African-American and Hispanic mothers. *Journal of Applied Developmental Psychology, 26(2).* 149-170.

Hughes, D. (2003). Correlates of African American and Latino parents' messages to children about ethnicity and race: A comparative study of racial socialization. *American Journal of Community Psychology, 31(1-2).* 15-33.

Ispa, J., Fine, M., Halgunseth, L., Harper, S., Robinson, J., Boyce, L., Brooks-Gunn, J., & Brady-Smith, C. (2004). Maternal intrusiveness, maternal warmth, and mother-toddler relationship outcomes: variations across low-income ethnic and acculturation groups. *Child Development, 75 (6).* 1613-1631.

Johnson, D. (2002). Adoption and the effect on children's development. *Early Human Development,68(1)*. 39-54.

Johnson, M., & Karmiloff-Smith, A.(2004). Neuroscience perspectives on infant development. In G. Bremner, & A. Slater, (Eds.) *Theories of infant development* (pp. 121-141). Malden, MA: Blackwell Publishing.

Kaufman, J., & Charney, D. (2001). Effects of early stress on brain structure and function: Implications for understanding the relationship between child maltreatment and depression. *Development and Psychopathology. Special Issue: Stress and development: Biological and psychological consequences, 13(3)*. 451-471.

Koenen, K., Moffitt, T., Caspi, Avshalom, Taylor, A., & Purcell, S. (2003). Domestic violence is associated with environmental suppression of IQ in young children. *Development and Psychopathology.* (15). 297-311.

Kohlberg, L. (1987). *Child psychology and childhood education: A cognitive developmental view.* New York: Longman.

Koverola, C., Papas, M., Pitts, S., Murtaugh, C., Black, M., & Dubowitz, H. (2005). Longitudinal investigation of the relationship among maternal victimization, depressive symptoms, social support, and children's behavior and development. *Journal of Interpersonal Violence, 20(12)*. 1523-1546.

Levy, T.L. & Orlans, M. (1998). *Attachment, Trauma and Healing, Understanding and Treating Attachment Disorder in Children and Families.* Washington, DC: Child Welfare League of American Press, p.19-20.

Lytton, H. (2000). Toward of model of family-environmental and child-biological influences on development. *Developmental Review, 20 (1)*. 150-179.

Maccoby, E. (1980). *Social Development: Psychological Growth and the Parent-Child Relationship.* New York: Harcourt Brace Jovanovich.

MacWhinney, B. (2005). Language evolution and human development. In B. Ellis, & D. Bjorklund,(Eds.) *Origins of the social mind: Evolutionary psychology and child development* (pp. 383-410). New York: Guilford Press.

Mahler, M. (1974). Symbiosis and individuation: The psychological birth of the human infant. *Psychoanalytic Study of the Child, 28.*

Margolin, G., Oliver, P. & Medina, A. (2001). Conceptual issues in understanding the relation between interparental conflict and child adjustment: Integrating developmental psychopathology and risk/resilience perspectives. In J. Grych, & F. Fincham,(Eds.) *Interparental conflict and child development: Theory, research, and applications* (pp. 9-38). New York: Cambridge University Press.

McCloskey, L., Jose Figueredo, A., & Koss, M. (1995). The effects of systemic family violence on children's mental health. *Child Development*, 66, 1239-1261.

McEwen, B. (2003). Early Life Influences on Life-Long Patterns of Behavior and Health. *Mental Retardation and Developmental Disabilities Research Reviews.* (9). 149-154.

McIntosh, J. (2003). Children Living with Domestic Violence: Research Foundations for Early Intervention. *Journal of Family Studies, 9(2).* 219-234.

Mead, M. (1967). The life cycle and its variations: The division of roles. *Daedalus: Journal of the American Academy of Arts & Sciences, 96 (3).* 871-875.

Moore, J. G., Galcius, A., & Pettican, K. (1981). Emotional risk to children caught in violent marital conflict - The Basildon treatment project. *Child Abuse and Neglect*, 5, 147-152.

Nelson, C. (2003). Can We Develop a Neurobiological Model of Human Social-Emotional Development? Integrative Thoughts on the effects of Separation on Parent-Child Interactions. *New York Academy of Sciences.* (1008). 48-54.

Newman, B.M. & Newman, P.R. (1995). *Development Through Life- A Psychosocial Approach.* Pacific Grove, CA: Brooks/Cole Publishing Co.

Okimoto, J. (2001). The appeal cycle in three cultures: An exploratory comparison of child development. *Journal of the American Psychoanalytic Association, 49(1).* 187-215.

Osofsky, J. (2004). Community Outreach for Children Exposed to Violence. *Infant Mental Health Journal. Special Issue: Amsterdam World Congress: Plenary Papers, 25(5).* 478-487.

Penza, K. M., Heim, C., & Nemeroff, C. B. (2003). Neurobiological effects of childhood abuse: implications for the pathophysiology of depression and anxiety. *Archives of Women's Mental Health.* (6). 15-22.

Perry, B.D. For: In Geffner, B. (Ed.) The Cost of Child Maltreatment: Who Pays? We All Do. Haworth Press. Retrieved 11/29/2005: http://www.childtrauma.org/ctamaterials/Neuroarcheology.asp

Perry, B.D. & Pollard, D. (1997). Altered brain development following global neglect in early childhood. *Neuroscience: Proceedings from Annual Meeting,* New Orleans. Retrieved 11/29/05: http://www.childtrauma.org/ctamaterials/Neuroarcheology.asp

Perry, B.D. (2001b). The neurodevelopmental impact of violence in childhood. In Schetky D & Benedek, E. (Eds.) Textbook of child and adolescent forensic psychiatry. Washington, D.C.: American Psychiatric Press, Inc. (221-238).

Perry, B.D. (2002). Childhood experience and expression of genetic potential: What childhood neglect tells us about nature and nurture. *Brain and Mind, 3,* 79-100.

Petchers, M. (1995). *Child maltreatment among children in battered mothers households.* Paper presented at the 4th International Family Violence Research Conference: Durham, NH.

Piaget, J. (1954). *The construction of reality in the child.* New York: Ballentine Books.

Piaget, J. (1963). *The origins of intelligence in children.* New York: Norton.

Piaget, J. (1968). *Judgement and reasoning in the child.* Totowa: Littlefield, Adams, & Co.

Piaget, J. (1969). *The child's conception of the world.* Totowa: Littlefield, Adams, & Co.

Ramey, S. (2002). The science and art of parenting. In J. Borkowski, S. Ramey, & M. Bristol-Power,(Eds.) *Parenting and the child's world: Influences on academic, intellectual, and social-emotional development. Monographs in parenting.* (pp. 47-71). Mahwah, NJ: Lawrence Erlbaum Associates.

Roer-Strier, D. (2001). Reducing risk for children in changing cultural contexts: Recommendations for intervention and training. *Child Abuse & Neglect, 25(2).* 231-248.

Schore, A.N. (2003). *Affect Regulation and Repair of the Self.* New York, NY: WW Norton & Co.

Schuder, M., & Lyons-Ruth, K.(2004). "Hidden Trauma" in Infancy: Attachment, Fearful Arousal, and Early Dysfunction of the Stress Response System. In J. Osofsky,(Ed.) *Young children and trauma: Intervention and treatment* (pp. 69-104). New York: Guilford Press.

Solms, M. & Turnbull, O. (2002). *The Brain and the Inner World: An Introduction to the Neuroscience of Subjective Experience.* New York: Other Press.

Stern, D. (1985). *Interpersonal world of the infant.* New York: Basic Books.

Streeck-Fischer, A., & van der Kolk, B. (2000). Down will come baby, cradle and all: Diagnostic and therapeutic implications of chronic trauma on child development. *Australian and New Zealand Journal of Psychiatry, 34(6).* 903-918.

Suh, E. & Abel, E.M. (1990). The impact of spousal violence on the children of the abused. *Journal of Independent Social Work, 4(4),* 27-34.

Vasterling, J. & Brewin, C. (Eds.) (2005). *Neuropsychology of PTSD: Biological, Cognitive and Clinical Perspective.* New York: The Guilford Press.

Weber, Deborah A. and Reynolds, Cecil R. (2004). Clinical Perspectives on Neurobiological Effects of Psychological Trauma. *Neuropsychology Review. 14* (2). 115-129.

Wekerle, C., & Wolfe, D. (2003).Child maltreatment. In E. Mash, & R. Barkley, (Eds.) *Child psychopathology (2nd ed.)*(pp. 632-684). New York: Guilford Press.

Wheeler, P. (2003). Shaken Baby Syndrome-An Introduction to the Literature. *Child Abuse Review, 2003, 12(6).* 401-415.

Winnicott, D. W. (1986). The theory of the parent-infant relationship. In P. Buckley (Ed.), *Essential papers on object relations. Essential papers in psychoanalysis.* (pp. 233-253). New York: New York University Press.

Wolfe, D. A. , Jaffe, P., Wilson, S.K., & Zak, L. (1985). Child of battered women: The relation of child behavior to family violence and maternal stress. *Journal of Consulting and Clinical Psychology,* 53 (5), 657-665.

Woolf, A., Shane, H., Kenna, M., & Allison, K.(Eds.).(2001).*The Children's Hospital guide to your child's health and development.* Cambridge, MA: Perseus Publishing.

www.ingramcontent.com/pod-product-compliance
Lightning Source LLC
Chambersburg PA
CBHW031257090426
42742CB00007B/488